How to Succeed in
Sales and Business

A Winners Mindset

Ryan Durden

Introduction

This Special edition includes 7 Major Keys For Young Adults In Sales and Business and Momentum – Ryan Durden's Journey to Success.

There are two ways to learn - through trial and error, or by learning from others (their mistakes and successes). The world is full of average people who accept mediocracy. This book is written for those who want more out of their lives through sales and business. Life isn't all about money, but it will provide you with the lifestyle you want for yourself, so it is important that we focus on it. However, just having a lot of money won't make you happy either. It's important that we strengthen our minds, so that when success does happen we are ready for it and we keep it, in all aspects of life. Its one thing to become successful it's another thing to remain successful.

I am currently on my journey to success - interviewing successful people all over the world and seeing what it is that makes them successful. Studying and learning the process so that I can put it all in one place, for you to take advantage of. Once I realized that success was a journey and not a destination, my whole mind state changed. There have been other inspirational books written on success, but none like this one. This book is full of information that will help anyone just starting, or already on their journey to success, achieve more, earn more, and live a better life.

The best book ever written on this subject is, *Think and Grow Rich* written by Napoleon Hill in 1937. I have been studying *Think and Grow Rich* for 17 years, and I consistently refer to the book and learn something new every time. Not only will this book give you some of the secrets that were unlocked in *Think and Grow Rich*, but it will also provide you with stories that are up to date with what's going on today, and some of the tactics the biggest guys in the industry like Grant Cardone use to gain prosperity and wealth.

The world is changing so fast that it's hard to keep up. The way we communicate has changed, technology is changing every day, and we are moving from a realistic society to a virtual society - in a hurry. People are using social media in ways that twenty years ago none of us would have ever imagined. In fact, Gary Vaynerchuck just wrote a book called *Crushing it*, where he shares his and other people's stories on how they became successful using different social media platforms.

It's what we do with our time that matters the most, and in Daymond John's book, *Rise and Grind*, he goes into detail on how our daily routines directly influence our success. He gives us his story and other stories on how their hustle and grind starts bright and early and how they spend their time dedicated to whatever they are working on. Creating routines and not wasting any time.

Maybe you've tried to start your own company or had a sales job in the past, and it didn't work out. Maybe it did, and then you got laid off, and now you don't know what to do - you were busy building their company and forgot to build you, or your brand, in the process. Maybe you go out on the weekends, and you can't seem to resist temptation and end up getting fired from every job you ever get. Maybe you have a sales job now, or you own your own business, and your sales are not where you want them to be. This may be because you aren't focusing on the right things. Maybe you struggle with getting along with people or have a hard time communicating or talking in front of people. Or maybe you just don't know how to get started.

This book was designed to help and inspire young people who are in sales or want to start their own business, reach the next level in their career while battling temptations that we face as young people in business today. By developing a strong mindset, we can achieve anything in life. As a continued student of personal development, business, and sales, I've learned that the more you share with others, the more you get back in return, especially if you aren't expecting anything in return at all. That's why I want to share more of my story, and stories of others that will move you, inspire you and help you build a mindset that will lead you to success.

The Seven Major Keys

There are seven major keys that you must possess when mastering your mindset to win in sales and business. This book will give you the definition of the seven keys to get your mind right, seven daily affirmations, five popular quotes specific to each major key, and an action section so you can start now. Sales and business are both an art form that anyone, no matter their background, can master and make a good living for themselves, and their families. You can be a student right out of college or high school, a high school dropout, or have a PhD in business, but when it comes to sales, it's all about who can produce the numbers. Anyone can become a millionaire or at least create a decent living using the art of sales and business. In sales, your titles and certificates don't matter, what matters is, if that person liked you or get attracted to you and they buy from you. It's a game of numbers; it's about how many people you can communicate with and in the end, convince to take the action. If you work on mastering these seven major keys, your world of possibilities is endless. The sales industry is not for everybody, but it is for anybody. What I mean by that is, anyone can do it, but a lot of people just don't want to take the time to learn how, and it's not the most honorable job in the world. For decades, sales people have had bad raps, from car salesman to telemarketers, but in every company, it's the sales people that get paid the most money. Some salespeople can be pushy, and some can seem desperate, the key to becoming good at sales is flipping the script, and caring about what the customer wants, instead of acting on your own agenda. If you are in sales, or just started your own business, and need to get to that next level, this book was made just for you. If you think that you can go into business for yourself without learning how to make sales, you will fail. While eighty percent of businesses make it past their first year, only half of them make it past their fifth year. The myth that ninety percent of businesses fail within their first year is false and just another myth to prevent you from capitalizing.

I recommend taking notes, highlighting key words and sections, and writing down anything and everything that comes to your mind while reading this book. Before moving on, get your success journal ready to make your notes.

     I.   **CONFIDENCE**
    II.   **LAW OF ATTRACTION**
   III.   **TRUST**
   IV.   **HUSTLE**
    V.   **COMMUNICATE**
   VI.   **NO FEAR**
  VII.   **PRIORITIZE**

(When thinking of the seven keys, use this analogy to help you remember them)

CHANGING LIVES THROUGH HUSTLE CREATES NEW PROSPECTS

In this book, I will cover each major key, defining each one, an affirmation that you can include in your daily affirmations, a back story, a how-to section, and quotes from celebrities, athletes, and other influential people. You must start thinking of yourself as a *business,* starting now. The fastest way to lose or fail is to give up. If you want to become successful in your business or sales, follow the guidelines and requirements outlined in this book. Only YOU have the power to change the outcome of your life, start today by acting now.

Table of Contents

Table of Contents

KEY 1 - Build Self Confidence

"Inaction breeds doubt and fear. Action breeds confidence and courage. If you want to conquer fear, do not sit at home and think about it. Go out and get busy."

- Dale Carnegie

Definition

Self Confidence - A feeling of trust in one's own abilities, qualities, and judgments.

Affirmation.

I am a well liked confident person, and I see myself with the success eye of now and have discarded the failure eye of my future. I am confident in all that I do, and I believe in myself!

Where do You Start?

Confidence is where it all starts when you are trying to create a positive mindset to attain success. It is the main door that leads to all success stories. You must have confidence in yourself to drive a car, to interview for a position, to graduate college, but most importantly, you must have the confidence to go out into the world, and sometimes it isn't an easy task, especially on your own. Confidence is a skill that can be learned and mastered by anyone who wants to learn. You may be a shy person who really doesn't like to talk in front of people, but by repetition and practice, you can become confident in anything.

Confidence mixed with repetition is a strong force, and when you think of yourself to be the best, the rest of the world will follow. It won't happen overnight, but with practice and positive reinforcement, it can be done. Perception is everything and how you perceive yourself dictates whether the world will follow you. Be careful not to be overconfident in your decisions. Make sure you are prioritizing and thinking right before acting.

Confidence alone is not enough; you must practice and work every day at your craft. You can have all the confidence in the world, and if you play Lebron James one on one, most likely you will not win. Confidence is just the starting point. Lebron James was born with natural abilities, but those natural abilities were fueled by confidence at an early age. Everyone has their own natural abilities, and our jobs as human beings are to identify what those abilities are and work on them to become the best version of us we can be.

People want to do business with someone they respect, someone who's authentic and has a lot of energy. They want someone with confidence, they need you to believe in yourself, before they can believe in you. To gain confidence, you must have swag. Swag is when you walk and talk in a confident way, and many perceive it as arrogant or cocky. They are going to look at you differently, they are going to say you are fake and that you aren't really that person you are trying to be. They are going to hate on you and tell you, you are crazy, you're a dreamer and you'll never accomplish what you set out to do. Those people don't matter right now. What matters to you right now is to create a mindset that is going to bring you to the next level. When you think like an average person, you will get average results. We need the average people to make the economy work, so you don't have to be one. Being average is a choice and so is being successful. Some people want to be average, some people love the security of a salary, and knowing what's coming in every month. Unless you are a successful lawyer or doctor, or a professional athlete, you won't become rich on a salary. You will become rich based on your results, how business savvy you are, and your willingness to get better. You will only get better if you believe in yourself. When you light the fire inside of you, you can shed light on the entire world.

Growing up, self-confidence was always a problem. I lived in a separated home and my father was always moving from city to city to provide for us. I went to four elementary schools, so I couldn't create close relationships with any of my peers. To gain confidence, you must get into a routine, and my routine was consistently changing. Being mixed, other kids couldn't really relate to me. I wasn't black enough to hang out with the black kids and too black to hang out with the white kids. I really didn't feel like I had a place, at school or at home. I was smaller than most and I was an average athlete. I felt left out, and I didn't fit in anywhere. In my mind, I was never going to be able to have that feeling of acceptance. I looked for acceptance anywhere I could. I became insecure and just started to let life happen to me. I didn't know what was happening at the time, but I was angry at a situation that I had no control over. As children, we are put into situations we have can't control. And once you clock eighteen, there are no more excuses. We are given or at least expected to have complete control on how we want our lives to turn out. What I wish I would have known growing up, was that it wasn't the things that were happening to me, it was how I reacted to those problems that led to my own problems.

When I was in junior high, I would get into fights, hang out with the bad kids, ditch school, and my grades were horrible. My dad and my stepmom took me out of public school and enrolled me in a private Christian school. There I learned discipline and was able to meet my best friend Iain who is now the Godfather to my children. Iain was the kid who got straight A's, was athletic, and people liked him. When I first arrived at the private school, Iain saw me as a threat. I felt his eyes scold me as I walked around campus, again not knowing anyone. Eventually, we started hanging out and found out we had a lot in common. I analyzed what he did and how he handled situations. I saw that his abilities to do the things he was able to do, were on the belief he had in himself and he was sure of himself. After attending UCLA and Emory Law School, He is now working in Los Angeles, pursuing his dreams and becoming the best person he can be. Prior to attending the private school, I saw myself as a failure. But when I saw what self-confidence did to Iain, I was sold that I had to start thinking of myself differently.

Going into high school, I was still smaller than most of my peers and I still struggled with confidence. But as time went by, I was starting to gain some confidence, by finding acceptance from my peers through sports and my parents by getting good grades in school. By my junior year, I was now tall, strong, and I had all the confidence in the world. My senior year after the football season, things started to go downhill again. On a vacation I took, someone that I looked up to and was supposed to have my best interest in mind offered to give me drugs. I thought if this person engages in it and is offering it to me, then it's not that bad. At the time, I never saw drugs or even heard about it for that matter. I went back to school and two weeks later, my old self found its way back into my life through drugs. I started hanging out with the wrong crowd again, started using drugs, and drinking every day. One day I was drinking at the park with some friends after school, and as we were leaving, two cop cars pulled up behind me, they pulled us out of the car and have me arrested for underage drinking and DUI. I felt like I let everyone down, I lost my car and the trust of my parents. I lost all the confidence I built in those three years of high school. In my senior year, I only had two classes in the day. I spent my afternoons doing drugs, selling drugs, and trying to impress girls. I wasn't where I wanted to be, but I really didn't care at the time. I was so bad I didn't want to be around family or my real friends. I stayed on the streets sometimes throughout the entire night, looking to get into trouble. I didn't care what happened to me at that point in my life. I turned into a good athlete and could have played football in college and maybe beyond, but I stopped believing in myself, and I gave up. I used the DUI as an excuse, instead of treating it like a lesson. I thought it was the end of the road for me, so I just threw it in the trowel. I didn't take any responsibility for how my life was turning out, it was always someone else's fault.

My father was able to talk me into going to college, but I really didn't want to go. I didn't believe in myself as he believed in me. He drove me up to Northern California to attend Cal

State Stanislaus, and I lived in the dorms. I ended up not going to any classes and just hanging out in the dorms feeling sorry for myself for messing up my life, not seeing the opportunity that my father set right in front of me. I was in a haze; I was drinking and doing drugs and ended up getting arrested again and doing three months in county jail. I was heading down a spiral staircase to my demise as a human being. I went back to San Diego and still felt sorry for myself. I didn't believe that I could make things better for myself. I was way off track, and I didn't know what I was going to do with the rest of my life. I ended up leaving San Diego on my own terms and wanted to start my life over afresh.

I moved to Arizona with some friends, got into sales, and I started to get good at it. I worked on my craft and I got into a routine. I enrolled back in school and graduated with a degree in media arts. I stayed back in Arizona while my friends went back to San Diego. I was on my own, and now I wanted to prove to my parents that I wasn't a failure. I started looking at myself differently. I had responsibilities and I wanted a better life for myself. I wasn't drinking all the time or using drugs. I was focused on myself and I had goals. I worked out every day, I had good relationships with my family and my friends, and overall, I was happy. I started to set goals for myself, I started talking to people, I stopped doing drugs, I started to focus on my affirmations and studied my ass off at work. Before, I was afraid of failure, I was afraid that I would sabotage myself. I became fearless, I took risks that I thought would better my life instead of hindering it. By doing so, I was able to approach my wife, convince her I was the one, and was able to start a family. This is all because my confidence grew, and I started winning. Eleven years later, my wife and I are still together. I took my confidence and I'm now teaching others how to build confidence and provide for their families. It feels good and I now have the confidence to accomplish my goals and see through anything life throws at me. You can gain self-confidence by believing in yourself, following the steps I have written out for you, and by acting now.

When you are constantly working on getting better, you can achieve anything. If you are doing things that you aren't proud of, that hinders the relationships between you and your friends or family; you should rethink your priorities. Confidence is where it all starts, and you must be confident in yourself before you can proceed to succeed. Get it right with yourself, prove to yourself that you are capable of anything and use that confidence to get started on your dreams of becoming the best you   can   possibly   be.

How to gain self-confidence

Self-confidence starts with how you perceive yourself. If you see yourself as a failure, everyone else sees you as a failure. Train your mind to believe that you are confident. Write out at least 10 affirmations and include I am confident in all that I do in your listed affirmations. You must visualize the win beforehand, and you will start to see yourself as confident.

Take care of yourself. Shave, do your hair, or get a haircut. Dress for success - when you look in the mirror, you should be proud to step out of the house. Work out; you don't have to become a bodybuilder, a 30-minute a day work out goes a long way.

First impressions are important. Make sure you are doing everything in your power to make an outstanding first impression.

Walk with your chest out. If you're in an office or place of work, stand up, and move around. Be bold and talk with conviction.

Get into a routine. Write out your daily routine and include time to learn, workout, make income, and being with family.

Fill your mind with the knowledge that will help you grow. Invest in personal development books, audios, and videos. You'll start feeling good, and you'll start to learn new strategies that you could apply in your daily life.

Money isn't everything, but it's what keeps our economy on the go. And while money doesn't buy happiness, it's the resource necessary to make a positive impact on the world. Increase your income without jeopardizing your happiness, and you will start feeling better about yourself.

Gain knowledge. The more knowledge you have, the more confident you'll become. If you don't know what you are talking about, you'll look stupid, and you end up dispersing wrong information. If you don't know something, keep mute, or go in search of knowledge and get immersed before speaking.

Forget your fears. Fear is just an emotion. Emotions are direct consequences of our thoughts. Change the way you think about your fears. Challenge your fears and face them head-on and become fearless. Do things that you fear doing. If you fear heights, go skydiving or take a plane somewhere if you have the means. If you stay within your comfort zone, you will never grow. Step out of your comfort zone and face your fears, attack and fight the battle as if your life depends on it so that you can eat and feed yourself, and those around you.

Set smart goals. Set specific, measurable, attainable, relevant, and time-bound goals. Set yourself up for success. Make sure you can measure your progress, so you can keep growing. If you don't *hit the time you allotted yourself, don't get discouraged, don't stop until you've accomplished* your goal. And there will never be an end because your goal keeps growing as you accomplish it. Life is an unending battle that rewards you at every stage you succeed.

Confidence Quotes

"Our deepest fear is not that we are inadequate. Our deepest fear is that we are powerful beyond measure. It is our light, not our darkness, that most frightens us. We ask ourselves, 'Who am I to be brilliant, gorgeous, talented, fabulous?' Actually, who are you not to be?" **- Marianne Williamson**

"Low self-confidence isn't a life sentence. Self-confidence can be learned, practiced, and mastered - just like any other skill. Once you master it, everything in your life will change for the better." **- Barrie Davenport**

"Confidence is a habit that can be developed by acting as if you already had the confidence you desire to have." **- Brian Tracy**

"It is confidence in our bodies, minds, and spirits that allows us to keep looking for new adventures."- **Oprah Winfrey**

Conclusion

Confidence can be learned by educating ourselves, taking care of our bodies, and always preparing ourselves. We must face our fears and become leaders instead of followers. Set your own path and put it down on paper. You must have confidence to become successful in anything in life, and if you want to become a kick-ass salesperson, you must work on becoming confident in yourself before you go out into the field.

Key 2 - Law of Attraction

"Just decide who you are going to be, and how you're going to do it and the universe is going to get out of your way."

- Will Smith

Definition

Law of Attraction - The belief that if you focus your thoughts on positive thoughts or negative thoughts, that's what you'll attract into your life.

Affirmation

The world is out to help me succeed, and I am thankful for the life that I live. I spread happiness and joy to the world, and in return, I attract an abundance of wealth, health, and happiness.

How do you think?

In a recent interview I did with Carl Michel, bestselling author of *365 Daily Motivational Hip Hop quotes*, he said "I changed the status on my Instagram to bestselling author six months before I released my book." He believed in himself before anyone else did, he knew that he was a bestselling author before he even finished the book. Most successful people believe in the law of attraction to some degree. Even if they don't believe in it, it's still there. We attract whatever we think about.

You see it all the time, when times are tough, times are tough, right? It doesn't have to be like that anymore. You can use your thoughts to change the outcome of your life. By practicing the law of attraction, you can turn your life around 180 degrees for the better. There are a couple of ways to change your way of thinking. You can use methods of cognitive therapy by implementing cognitive reframing and cognitive restructuring. The word cognition means to know or perceive. If we know that we control our thoughts and our thoughts lead to our reality, think of the power and the life we would live if we learn to manipulate our mind to finding a positive outcome in every circumstance. The mind is a powerful tool and when used to do good and help other people, it connects with the universe and rewards you with good health, wealth, happiness, and lasting relationships.

As human beings, we all have emotions, but we must understand that our thoughts control our emotions, and our emotions lead to the way we react. We all have negative thoughts at some point in time but having too many negative thoughts can lead to mental illness like anxiety and depression. When understanding that we have the ability to change our mindset, we can save lives. Our own lives and the lives of others around us. On an average, there are about 125 suicides per day, so I'd say we have a big problem with the way we think. We must realize it early and try to change our way of thinking by working on it day in and day out. Staying positive is not an easy task; sometimes things don't go as planned, but we must remember that no matter what happens to us, there is always something positive that can be taken out of the situation.

The mind has three parts; the subconscious, the conscious, and the unconscious mind. Just ten percent of our mind is conscious, the subconscious takes up fifty to sixty percent of our mind, and the unconscious occupies the remaining thirty to forty percent. Our conscious mind carries out the duties. We are very aware of our conscious mind, and in fact, it's what controls our speech, physical movement, and our thoughts. Our conscious mind is like the internet; it's what connects the rest of the world with who you are. Our subconscious mind is where we store our information or data. We can tap into our subconscious mind any time by controlling our thoughts and surroundings. Our unconscious minds are like the long-lost files that we can't access.

To make the law of attraction work, we must know how the mind works. The subconscious mind controls the outcome of our lives. It controls our beliefs, what we learned in school, and everything that we programmed into our mind since we were kids. The key to making the law of attraction work is to reprogram your subconscious mind to the right way of thinking.

The gap between the rich and the middle class is expanding rapidly, and it has everything to do with the seven major keys, and what we are exposed to. To experience what the rich and famous have, we must study and practice what the rich and famous are doing. We must figure out their mindset, study their subconscious mind and how they think. We must reprogram our brains to believe that money is a tool, that we can use to help and lead people who need help in this world. We must stop believing the media hype that people with money

13

are evil people who don't pay taxes. We cannot fall into the trap of the divide created by the government. It doesn't matter if you are a democrat or a republican, if you are on a mission to provide for yourself and your family through sales and business, then we are on the same team. If you don't become rich in the next couple of decades, your family will be poor. In twenty years from now, there will no longer be three economic classes; we will have the rich and the poor. Which class will you be? It's up to you to make a choice. But as an unpaid for advice, decide quickly because you might be running out of time.

We must dream big - if you think big and have big goals, even if you don't reach your goals, you will be a lot better off than most. If you think average, you will become poor. Thinking big is mandatory to succeed in sales, and in business. We can't just think big; we must act big. That means we must take bigger action and put in more effort if we want to even come close to where we want to be. The law of attraction will only work if you act and work towards your goals, and the key is to map it out, so you can visualize it and think about it every day - it's not magic, its science. We become what we think about most, so repetition is the most important part of the law of attraction. It takes discipline, just like any other work out, and that's exactly what the law of attraction is, a workout for your mind. If you are a gym rat, you'll find that the law of attraction easy and will work for you if you can just add your financial and lifestyle goals into your work out. In business, it's about maximum effort; it's about who's willing to put in the most reps and work the hardest and smartest.

When I was fifteen, my grandfather wrote out my first set of affirmations and everything he wrote down, came into life. I am now working on my third set of affirmations. Any time I've succeeded at anything in my life, I saw it in my head before it took place. I lost my way a couple of times in my life, but luckily, I've always had my affirmations to fall back on. During my sophomore year in high school, my grandfather started helping and coaching my football team. He was a former NFL coach and brought some knowledge to the team. He made us close our eyes and visualize our assignments before every game and every practice. We ended up having a great season and to this day, I have players approach me and tell me how much of an impact that had on their lives. We have a conscious mind and a subconscious mind, and the key to making the law of attraction work in our favor is to reprogram our subconscious mind in the right direction. The conscious mind can only hold one thought at a time, your conscious mind is constantly observing what's going on around you. Your subconscious mind stores the data that we take in from our conscious minds. We must program our subconscious mind to store information that we want it to store. You can start practicing the law of attraction by following what I have written out for you and believing that the universe is here to help you succeed and not to fail. The law of attraction will help you manifest anything you want in your life. Whatever you put out, you are going to get it in return. You might be skeptical about the law of attraction but it's not just wishful thinking. Many celebrities and successful people have used and have given us proof that it's real. The most powerful men and women in the world used the law of attraction to get to where they are. Another moment that I used the law of attraction was when I opened my first business. In my head, before I even had the opportunity to start my own company, I saw exactly how I was going to have it set up. I didn't know how it was going to happen, but it did. One day, my boss set up a conference call with all the agents, and he made it known to us all that we no longer had our jobs. He said you have two options: one, to take a severance paycheck or two, start our own office. I was the only one out of ten to choose to open my own office. I already knew I wanted my own office, but now I knew how. It was a blessing in disguise, and because I was mentally ready, the disguise was to my advantage. I knew it was a blessing the whole time. I wasn't scared of opening my own office, and I was excited and eager to start.

How to use the law of attraction

Be protective of what you allow into your brain, surround yourself with positive people and a positive environment, listen to positive music, and watch inspirational movies.

When something happens in your life, there are two ways to look at it.

Here is an example of two people getting a flat tire on the same day at the same time, while on their way to work.

Daniel	Tony
Negative Thinker	**Positive Thinker**

Thought: This day is going to suck	Thought: Oh well, the day can only get better.
Emotion: Angry	Emotion: Confident
Action: Calls his job place and tells his boss he has a flat tire and he won't be able to make it. Boss says he's had too many absences and fires him.	Action: Calls his job place and says he'll be a little late, changes his tire, goes into work. He finally gets promoted.

Identify what your negative thoughts are. Write down all your negative thoughts and try to find something positive that you can take out of it. There will always be a positive to every negative.

Put pictures around your house or office that represents or reminds you of your dreams, motivational quotes, and goals. If you are constantly looking at positive pictures, you are creating positive vibes.

Visualize, create a dream board, and meditate. Create time in your day to view yourself where you want to be.

Dream big, don't settle for mediocre. If you want a boat, a mansion, and jet skis, make sure you put that in your affirmations.

Spread positive vibes, smile, laugh and be happy. Be supportive to others around you and give back. Show random acts of kindness.

Share your goals with others. Get your dreams out there, tell it to everyone. They may not believe you at first, but if you tell enough people and put it out into the universe, they will start to believe you because the universe will hear you and in return, you will accomplish your dreams.

Start reading and listening to audios to help you attract the lifestyle you want. If you turn your car into drive time university, your subconscious mind will pick up bits and pieces. Read for at least 30 minutes a day on books that will help you succeed.

Create your success journal. Include your affirmations, your wish list, and a to-do list. Cut out pictures in magazines or print them off and glue them in the journal. Write down all your goals and create an action plan for each goal. Each goal must have ten action steps. Write down everything you are grateful for.

Attraction Quotes

"The law of attraction is a law, like the law of gravity, its physics." - **Kevin Trudeau**

"See the things that you want as already yours. Know that they will come to you at need. Then let them come. Don't fret and worry about them. Don't think about your lack of them. Think of them as yours, as belonging to you, as already in your possession." – **Robert Collier**

"What things soever ye desire, when ye pray, believe that ye receive them, and ye shall have them." – **Mark 11:24**

"Impossible is just a big word thrown around by small men who find it easier to live in the world they've been given than to explore the power they have to change it. Impossible is not a fact. It's an opinion.

Impossible is not a declaration. It's a dare. Impossible is potential. Impossible is temporary. Impossible is nothing." **– Muhammad Ali**

Conclusion

You can use the law of attraction to attract good things or bad things into your life; it's all about how you think. Change your negative thoughts into positive thoughts, anytime you think of a negative thought, get hold of yourself, and correct it. Understand how the mind works and use it to your advantage. Create your goals and repeat them over and over, at least twice a day consistently until you've accomplished all your goals. Understand that it's a process and it won't happen overnight, it may not even happen in five years, but don't give up, it could happen tomorrow.

OPEN TO ACCEPTING ALL
FORMS OF ABUNDANCE
THE UNIVERSE HAS
TO OFFER ME.

19

Key 3 - Trust

"It takes twenty years to build a reputation and five minutes to ruin it."

- Warren Buffett

Definition

Trustworthy - When you can be relied on as honest or truthful.

Affirmation

I am a trustworthy and loyal person, people believe in me. I am building long-lasting relationships in business and my personal life.

How can I trust you?

The only way someone will ever buy from you, go into business with you, or enter a relationship with you, is if they trust you. Trust is key to any relationship, business or personal. People will buy from you most of the time if they like you, but they will buy from you all the time if they trust you wholeheartedly.

There are four different types of trust, and each type has a different level of trustworthiness. The first is credibility - if you come recommended or have credentials to show you know what you are selling or talking about, you automatically gain the trust of that person, for that specific topic. This doesn't mean that they trust you with their life, but it does mean you have more of a chance to sell them a service or a product. The second type is being reliable with your actions. People trust other people who are reliable and do what they say they are going to do. If you consistently do as you say, it becomes a pattern and the other person automatically starts to believe what you say. This person will trust you when you say you're going to do something, they know they can rely on you for almost anything. The third reason is because they have a sense of security with you, they've known you for a long time and they can trust you with their secrets. They are intimate with you and while they might trust you with their secrets, they may not trust your actions. They know you have good intentions and that you mean well, but you may not demonstrate reliability. This type of trust is common in most families. The fourth type of trust is focus, which just means you show genuine interest in the other person, and you pay attention to every word they are saying. When you respond to a person, you respond to what they are asking or saying, not to what you are feeling, or what happened to you that was similar. A lot of people will respond to a person with a similar story of their own, completely blowing off what the other person was talking about. When you are genuinely interested in what other people are saying, and asking questions, they get a sense that you care about what they are saying, and you begin to build rapport. Rapport comes from understanding each other's point of view, and when you completely blow off what others are saying without giving what they said attention, you lose their trust.

Being loyal is mandatory in business; you must be loyal to your company, your partners, and employees. Being loyal means to be faithful, being true to the facts, and showing genuine and undeniable support. Remember that the company must come first, then the partners, and then the employees. There are levels of loyalty; if you want to grow your business, then you need to have the most focus on your business. If you are loyal to the company and believe in the company wholeheartedly, you will give maximum effort and gain the trust of all of those around you. When an employee trusts a company, it makes the journey a lot smoother, and it creates synergy. In business, synergy is necessary because everyone feeds off each other, and motivates each other to do better because they all believe in the same thing, they all have the same goal, and they are working together to accomplish that goal. As sales professionals, we also must be loyal to our customers, without the customer, you wouldn't have a business. They are who you are serving, and if you get the customer to trust you, and you keep that trust, you have a lifelong customer.

To be good at business, you must have your home in order too - your relationships outside of work will affect the way you do business. A couple of years back, I lost the trust of my wife. The result was, she left me and took my kids. I wanted my family back so bad, that I started studying the subject of trust, and knew that if I could gain her trust back, I could win my family back. By genuinely wanting to be with her, and by doing everything I told my wife I was going to do, I was able to win her back and gain her trust. By continuously reassuring her that I am reliable, with my actions and by keeping my word, her trust in me continues to grow. When I said I was going to do something, I made sure that I did, and as fast as I possibly could. It took two years until she finally started to trust me again, but in those two years, I became a student of trust and spent money on videos and books to help win her back. The biggest thing that I took out of those two years is, it takes time and maximum effort if you want to gain someone's trust, once you lose it. Once you have that person's trust, do everything you can to keep it.

As a teenager, I made some bad choices, and I lost the trust of everyone around me. It took a long time to gain some of that trust back, and it wasn't easy. I started selling when I was eighteen, and I have made thousands of sales, but nobody that I knew personally would ever buy from me. At first, I was a little upset, but after a while, I started to understand why they didn't. I was so unreliable in my early life, so why would they trust what I was selling. They had a perception of me running the streets, not as a business person. Luckily, I only knew a handful of people and was able to build new relationships with other people and keep their trust. The people in my past already had a perception of who I was at that time, but people change. That's the whole point of this book; people can change and become trustworthy. It's all a state of mind and one's principles.

People will trust you if you keep your word time and time again. I have friends and family members that I wouldn't trust with my finances or involve them in my business, but I trust them with my deepest darkest secrets. So, to gain the trust of someone you are trying to persuade, make sure you keep your word and prove your trustworthiness as early as possible. You only have about five minutes of stage time, so you must prove your trustworthiness fast. The way you do that is by building credibility, ask open-ended questions and be genuinely interested in the person. We give off vibes and if your intentions are good, and your communication skills are on point, then people will trust what you are saying. Don't be the snake oil salesman or the person who sells products that don't work. Find a reputable product or service you can stand by and feel good about when going to sleep at night. Keep your conscious mind clean and your head high, because when you have confidence mixed with positive thoughts, great communication skills, and you put in the work, people will start to believe you, and you will have unlocked key number three.

How to Build Trust

Industry Knowledge

Know your industry inside out, and don't stop learning. Stay up to date with what is going on in your industry. Take at least twenty minutes a day to learn something new in your industry.

Product knowledge

Know what you're selling. If you want to gain the trust of a customer, you must know what your product does. Use the product and become your own customer. If you want people to believe in your product, you must believe in it. How are you going to sell something that you don't even know or use?

Market knowledge.

Be honest at all times and follow through with what you say you are going to do. It's the little things that you lie about that causes people not to trust you.

When you lie consistently, you start to give off a vibe that can easily be read. Start being honest with yourself and others, and you will gain their trust.

Be direct, make sure the customers know if they are wrong, and find a polite way to correct them. Look at all angles and explore them, don't be close-minded. Let them know what you or your product can do and what you and your product can't do. When correcting them make sure you don't disagree with them, but you wanted to make sure that they had the right information. Find a solution together with the person, research on your phone, or on the computer.

Pay attention to what the customer is saying, listen to everything they say and acknowledge by engaging in asking questions.

Be loyal to those around you, show support and have faith in your business and personal partners. If someone is loyal they will eventually come back around; if they don't, you shouldn't waste your time with them anyway.

Trust yourself before you trust anyone else, and no one will trust you if you don't believe in yourself, stay confident.

Trust Quotes

"It is true that integrity alone won't make you a leader, but without integrity you will never be one." **- Zig Ziglar**

"Be true to yourself, stay focused and stay you, take advice from other folks, use what you can, but never mind what is not for you. For the most part, trust yourself and believe in what you are doing." - **Musiq Soulchild**

"To build a long-term, successful enterprise, when you don't close a sale, open a relationship." **-Patricia Fripp**

"We're never so vulnerable when we trust someone. But paradoxically, if we cannot trust, neither can we find love or joy." - **Walter Anderson**

Conclusion

There are four different levels of trust, and to become a master of sales and business, you must master all four levels. You must be credible, reliable, secure, and you must focus your attention on your audience. You must trust in yourself before you can gain the trust of others. Keep the trust of those who are closest to you, be loyal, and show respect to your business partners and life partners as well. Building trust takes time, and you may not gain the trust of a prospect the first time around, keep your word, and you'll keep your trust.

Key 4 - Hustle

"Smart work will never replace hard work; it only supplements it."
- Gary Vaynerchuk

Definition
Hustle - To give it everything you've got to accomplish a goal.

Affirmation

I am doing everything in my power to accomplish my goals; I am a hustler, I'm pushing myself to my limits and getting better every day.

Are you maximizing your efforts?

Many people get the wrong idea when I say I'm a hustler. They picture a drug dealer, or someone trying to cheat or swindle other people. In my view, a hustler is someone who gives it all they've got to accomplish a goal. In sports, my coaches would always tell me to hustle; they would use the word hustle to motivate me to move faster. When I hear the word hustle, I hear my coaches yelling at me to pick up the pace.

There are going to be people who are smarter than you, who are stronger than you, and who are more talented than you are. None of those things are in your control, but what is, is your ability to out-work them or out-hustle them. You can become better at something by just applying yourself and giving it all you have, day in and day out. I know that if you put me in any position, I won't be good at it at first, but my ambition and

27

drive will eventually kick in and I'll become a master at it. You must have ambition; you must want to be good at something. If you don't have the heart, you can't have the hustle. You don't have to love what you are doing, but you have to love the process. You must love the challenge; if you aren't up for the challenge, you can just sit in front of the television all day, get fat and lazy, and watch your life pass you by.

Nothing in life comes easy; you must put in the work day in and day out until it eventually pays off. Work requires physical and mental stability, and if you aren't in the right state of mind, you must go back to your why and your affirmations to figure out what you want and why you want it. To hustle means to give it all you've got to get what you want. If you aren't willing to hustle for it, you don't deserve it. Deserve comes from the Latin word "service". If you can't offer a service that helps people solve their problem, you don't deserve to succeed.

When you have huge goals and dreams, people will think you are crazy, and people will tell you that you are stupid. The thing is, your dream was put into your heart, not theirs, and only you can envision that was put into you. Only you know what it will take to accomplish that dream. The only way you will be able to become the best at anything is to hustle. Being a hustler is a good thing; it means you are taking care of yourself, your family, helping the economy grow, and offering a service that helps people. Become a hustler and you will increase your chances of success. I was an average athlete but every coach that I had, said I had a heart. I was always smaller than most, but my effort stood out more than everything else. Even though I wasn't the fastest, I always competed for that number one spot. I believed in myself before anyone else believed in me. I knew I didn't have the natural ability like my classmate in high school, Reggie Bush. Reggie had it all; the speed, the strength, and the brains. Even though Reggie worked hard at his profession, it came easy to him. Most people aren't like that and that's why only one percent of kids that play youth sports make it to play professionally. In that one percent, there are people that weren't born with natural abilities, they had to work twice as hard to get to where they are. A good example is Allan Iverson. Yes, he had tremendous amount of talent. But he was a regular size human being playing a game with giants. He didn't let his size, his race, or life circumstances affect is hustle. He had a goal to become a professional athlete and provide for his family and he did just that. Despite all his hardships, his hustle got him to where he wanted to be. There are so many people in the world with tremendous amounts of hustle. Don't be lazy; if you have something that needs to get done to get you to the next level, set an alarm and attack it. I have friends and family members that say and do anything and everything to get out of doing work. Their mindset is set, just to get by, they have no goals and they are in the same spot they started out at eighteen years old. The difference between the person standing on the corner and the person in the highest building in the biggest city is their hustle. The guy in the office put in the hard work to get to where he is now. The man on the corner let his bad circumstances determine how his life turned out to be. It's not too late for the guy on the corner to make a change. While we still deal with prejudice and racism, it is a lot easier for anyone no matter your race, gender, religion, or tax bracket to become financially stable and live a life where money isn't an issue, if you hustle. If you work hard and never give up, you are bound to get what you set out for. You must grind day in and day out. Anyone can be a hustler, you only need to have the desire to win, and the work ethic to get it done.

The key is work harder and smarter than your peers and stands out. If you put in the work and continue to learn, you will eventually succeed. You must manage your time and make sure you are using every second, especially at work to get better and try to become the best at that position, so that you can generate an income for yourself and your family. We limit our minds to what we are exposed to. If you work your ass off, you'll be exposed to a world that you've never imagined. A hustler will always find a way to get the job done. A hustler doesn't make excuses. A hustler is the first one in the door in the morning and the last one out the door at the end of the day. A hustler doesn't take bathroom breaks five minutes before lunch. A hustler doesn't need to be micromanaged. A hustler is the type of person that I want to work with. Someone who do not find excuses to execute the task at hand and are consistent in their zone. Someone who wants to be legendary.

How to hustle

Don't let your circumstances determine how your life will turn out. Your race, gender, or religion has nothing to do with your hustle. Stop making excuses; the only reason you aren't a hustler yet is that you haven't tried.

30

Get in a zone, eliminate all distractions, cell phones, television, anything that can draw your attention off your work needs to be out of sight and out of mind.

Work out and eat right; a hustler needs energy. Be careful what you put in your body. Limit your alcohol use, and don't let it become a problem, and keep your eye on the prize.

Be persistent, don't let go of your dreams. It may take longer than you expect. That's okay, keep hustling. If you have your eyes set on your dream; your desire, ambition, and drive, will lead you to victory. Be a goal getter; if you see an opportunity, cease it and execute. Chase your dreams and never give up. It may take a year or a decade, don't stop until you reach your goal.

Get excited about what you are doing. Energy is key. People can tell if you are passionate about something. People feel the vibe you give off, and if you genuinely love the hustle, it doesn't matter what you're selling, they can sense the passion that lives in you.

Get it done quickly. If you have something that needs to get done, do it right and get it done in a timely manner. Don't take excessive breaks, do so only when it's necessary - outwork everyone. If you have to, only break for the bathroom and food.

Keep personal problems at home, don't bring your life drama to work. Sometimes, home life can spill into your work life. You must keep them separate. Use your work life as an escape from your home life.

Show up for work, not to socialize. High school is over; it's time to get to work. Your co-workers or employees don't care if you fail or succeed. Use your time wisely, don't spend time talking about things that won't make you better.

Focus on one thing at a time and don't quit until you have finished that task. Get in the zone; you can't get in the zone if you keep on switching tasks. Once you've accomplished a task, then and only then, move on to the next one.

Show up early and leave late. One, your superiors and co-workers will see the extra work you are putting in, and two, any extra work you put in, the better chance of success you will have. Be the first one on the job, get your day started before everyone else. Be the last one out the door; most people sit around waiting for that clock to say five o'clock. At five o'clock, you should make that one last phone call, knock on that one last door, greet that one last person, send out that last email, do whatever it takes to go the extra mile.

Hustle Quotes

"I just think a hustler's ambition is that I never stop. I started off hustling and said I'll never stop hustling. An ambitious hustler is the one to hustle the hustlers. When I grew up, my heroes were hustlers. Now I'm their hero." - **Young Jeezy**

"Whatever you do, work at it with all your heart, as working for the lord, not for human masters - **Colossians 3:23**

"Approach every situation with an 'in it to win it whatever it takes' mindset. Sound too aggressive? sorry but that is the outlook required to win nowadays."- **Grant Cardone**

*"I can't relate to lazy people; we don't speak the same language. I don't understand you." - **Kobe Bryant***

Conclusion

There are going to be people who are naturally more talented than you, but they won't get to where you are going, because they lack the hustle. Be obsessed with executing and completing goals. Get off your butt and do something. Happiness doesn't just show up at your doorstep one day; you must get up, get out, and go get it. If you want to become successful in sales and business, you must learn the art of the hustle. Keep your personal problems at home so that you can focus on what needs to get done, get in the zone, and get it done fast and get it done right. No matter what stands in your way, focus on your goal and execute it.

Key 5 - Communication

"Communication is a skill that you can learn. It's like riding a bicycle or typing. If you're willing to work at it, you can rapidly improve the quality of every part of your life."

– Brian Tracy

Definition

Communication – Means of sharing or exchanging information, news or ideas to other people.

Affirmation

I can effectively communicate and connect with people. I listen and genuinely care about others, and I am fully aware of my surroundings.

Are you listening?

Once you find the courage to become confident, and you understand the law of attraction by reprograming your mind to find a positive outcome in every situation, you must learn how to effectively communicate your ideas, information, and feelings to others. We must first understand ourselves, and how to communicate with ourselves, before we can understand how to communicate with others. To be an effective communicator, we must understand our own pains and sufferings, where they come from, and how to overcome them so that we can understand what makes us happy. We must find out what brings us pain, identify what we have been through in our lives, why we have thoughts of hate, frustration, or fear so that we can turn them into thoughts of happiness, success, and love. When we operate out of love versus out of hate, we will have the support of the universe, and all her fruits. If we don't know what suffering is, we won't understand what happiness is. Once we find out what makes us suffer, we will have a better understanding of what other people are going through, and when we understand the suffering of others, instead of trying to prove ourselves to others, people will see the authenticity and compassion you have for them.

To understand and communicate with other people, we must have the ability to listen. Listening effectively is not as easy as we think, we tend to turn off each other and say things that trigger the other person to lose attention during the conversation. For me, when I listen to others, and they say something negative, hateful, or if they complain about something, it triggers me to stop listening to them. I can't control what people say when I'm engaged in a conversation, I can only choose how I react. I believe that if I let bad thoughts into my mind, they will manifest into my reality. Sometimes, it's a good thing to block out the negative commentary, however, if you want to communicate something to that person, and you truly care about them, you will listen to what they have to say, so you can understand them and find a solution to make them happy. In business and sales, it's the same process. If you truly care about your clients and you are genuinely trying to understand them, then your chances of getting your point across to them will be much more effective

As humans, we must have contact with other humans. In prison, the worst form of punishment is solitary confinement. Why is that? Because we must interact with others to maintain our sanity. When dealing with people, we have a choice on how we want to communicate. We can come across genuine and good people, or fraudulent and bad people, but we have a choice on how we communicate with them. It's not how others treat you, it's how you respond and treat others that determines the outcome of your life. How we communicate with others makes all the difference in staying average or dominating our lives. Whether you are in sales or starting your first business, you must master communication with your clients, partners, co-workers, and your employees. Being in a digital age, we communicate through our phones, our computers, through emails, video, and social media. We must be careful with what we say when we text or email because our emotion is hard to tell without hearing or seeing the other person. Make sure you are double checking your texts and emails before sending them out and read them out loud to make sure that you are actually getting your correct view across. Use commas appropriately and be very detailed and particular in your choice of words. If you use the wrong word, and type something that you really didn't mean, people might get the wrong perception of who you are or who you want to be. I don't think we will ever lose the face-to-face communication, and if you can master it, and the new way we communicate through digital media, you will be on your way to becoming the best sales and business person you can be.

Communication is the gateway to each other's minds, and we must start thinking about what we say before we say it.

Words are powerful and meaningful, and if we start thinking before we speak, we can make a major impact on our lives and the lives around us.

When I started working in sales, I began to dress a lot nicer. I wore slacks with a button up shirt and a tie. I felt good when I went to work, it was like when I got dressed for work my confidence level skyrocketed, and I was able to talk to anyone. People started to say hi to me, talk to me, and I became approachable. I had very good training classes that I went through for a sales position that I started, and they taught me how to greet people I didn't know, ask questions, and have them sign a contract with me. When I started selling, I knew I had to become an effective communicator or I wouldn't get paid. I started to talk to people every day, qualifying them and selling them cell phones, making money, and having a good time, all because I had learned how to communicate with other people. I was coachable and in return, I was able to coach other people. I moved up quickly to become a location manager. I took what I learned in the cell phone industry and used it in every single job and business that I've gone into. It was the first thing I learned how to do when I started selling and the most important part to humanity. Communication helped me transform from a little lost boy, to a successful salesman and businessman. As a rookie salesman, I learned how to qualify my customers and ask questions to find a solution. I learned that I had to listen to them and really pay attention to what they needed. I learned that I had to give them a solution and I had to know what I was talking about. I studied the cell phones and I knew all the features to every phone. I was able to identify my customer based on how they dressed, looked, and acted, and I wasn't scared to greet anyone. I knew how to adapt to different types of people, and the more people I talked to, the more the chance of making money, so I tried to talk to every single person that walked by. I could talk to anyone, and I started to become a well-rounded salesman. I moved on to selling other products, but my main training has always fallen back on communication. Communication is important in every relationship. If you can't communicate with people, you are never going to accomplish your goals. Unless you want to become a hermit, you must be able to communicate with people. Get out and start meeting new people, there are so many different types of people in this world and each person has something that you can learn from.

A closed mouth doesn't get fed, and I learned that when I took a position at a job and I made over six figures my first year at 23 years old. My boss had a position lined up for someone in Philadelphia and at the last minute the person backed out. I had the confidence to approach my boss and ask for the position. I had to make him believe that I was the person who should go out to Philadelphia. He gladly offered me the position and that was a start to a whole different life for me. I went on straight commission, but the pay was awesome. I never wanted to get paid an hourly wage again. I was very passive at first and learned quickly that I had to get the job done there and now or it would never get done. I was signing three to four merchant accounts a day, talking to all different types of business owners, picking up new things each time. Eventually, I became a business owner, and applied all what I had learned from them to my business. I was able to ask them what their biggest successes were, and I asked if they had any advice for me. Almost every single time, not only would I get good advice, but I also close the deal. They saw I was more into learning and getting better, and the job as a credit card processing agent was just my how. I was able to create good relationships with some of the merchants that I signed up, and the best thing that I got out of them, was the knowledge that they all contributed to me, and helping me become a master at communication.

How to become an effective communicator

First impressions are very important. Within the first ten seconds, the person you are talking to has already made their opinion about you. Although we won't win the hearts of everyone, it's up to us to make a good first impression. Dress for success, and make sure you are ready for anything at any time. You never know when that next opportunity is going to show up.

Speak with confidence. If you aren't confident in what you are saying, people won't believe you. Before speaking, study and learn about what you are speaking about. If you want people to believe you, you must show them that you are serious and knowledgeable.

If you fear to communicate with someone, write a letter or an email, and make sure you get everything that you wanted to communicate to that person, written out. Before you send the letter, re-read it and study what you want to say to that person. You'll find that by writing it down and going over it, you'll gain the confidence that you need to communicate your message.

Use analogies to clearly paint a picture in their head of something they can relate to. An analogy is a comparison between two different things, that is used to explain or clarify a topic. For example, life is a marathon. Obviously, life isn't a race, but if we keep a steady and consistent pace, and not burn ourselves out early, we will reach the finish line, and succeed.

Build rapport. Try to find common ground with the person or audience you are talking to. People tend to like people who are like minded or who they want to be like. Find common interest like; sports, music, lifestyle, fashion, anything you can think of.

Listen. Be genuinely interested in what people are saying. Instead of replying with a comparison, have them elaborate on what they were talking about. Ask open-ended questions and make statements to find answers. For example, I see you are wearing a San Diego Padre's hat, are you from San Diego?

Don't assume. Make sure you are asking questions, so you don't misinterpret their meaning. If something doesn't make sense, ask questions, before you speak. You'll lose your audience fast if you start assuming. We have all heard the saying "don't assume, you'll make an ass out of you and me." Use the verbiage, what do you mean?

Be repetitive. Make sure that they understand exactly what your key points are. If you are putting together a presentation, make sure you include your key points at least three times, so it sticks in their heads.

Keep a good sense of humor. Don't be silly, be witty and funny. There is a difference between being funny and silly. Being silly, you are only funny to yourself, being funny is when those around you laugh at your joke. Use humor to connect with people; it loosens them up, and they listen. A good example is the comedians that talk politics, they loosen up their audience and put on a good show, but some of the best comedians will speak the truth, and make us think, at the same time as making us laugh.

Be present. If you are engaged in a conversation, give that person your full attention. Don't look at your phone, don't have wandering eyes. Look people in the eye when engaged in a face-to-face conversation. Shake your head implying yes as if you agreed with them. If you are engaged in a conversation over the phone, let them speak, agree, then make your point.

Before you engage in a planned meeting, visualize your meeting and write out how the conversation will go. The more you plan, the better chance of success you will have at getting your point across.

Reply immediately to the person you are communicating with. If they leave you a voicemail or an email, reply as soon as you can.

Always agree. Even if you don't agree, act like you do. Don't let your pride stand in the way of your dream. You have your sights set on something much greater. Look at it from their perspective and try to relate to them, instead of disagreeing. It doesn't mean that you believe what they are saying, it just means you understand where they are coming from. Never interrupt anyone, let them finish and once they are done talking, then voice your opinion. Interrupting and disagreeing will end up in a debate, argument, or loss of a deal.

Don't over talk and take out filler words like umm and umm. Practice this by recording yourself and training your brain to replace the filler word with pauses.

Be nice, but do not be a pushover. Show people you are kind, but you mean business. Smile and laugh more, be a happy person, people don't want to deal with you if you are angry or sad all the time.

Communication Quotes

"Great communication begins with connection. What makes us different from one another is so much less important than what makes us alike - we all long for acceptance and significance. When we recognize those needs in ourselves, we can better understand them in others, and that's when we can set aside our judgments and just hear." – **Oprah Winfrey**

"The difference between the right word and the almost right word is the difference between lightning and a lightning bug." - **Mark Twain**

"To listen well is as powerful a means of communication and influence as to talk well." - **John Marshall**

"Kind words can be short and easy to speak, but their echoes are truly endless." – **Mother Theresa**

Conclusion

To influence people, you must be able to communicate. Take care of your mind and body, study and be happy more. Give people your full attention and listen to what they are saying. Use analogies to paint a clear picture for your audience. Find a way to engage in conversation, don't be scared to approach people. Find common ground and have a genuine conversation with them. Dress sharp; first impressions go a long way. Never argue, look at things from other people's point of view.

KEY 6 - No Fear of Rejection

"Success is the ability to go from failure to failure without losing your enthusiasm."

– *Winston Churchill*

Definition

Fear - An emotion that is caused by a threat by something or someone, usually causing pain.

Rejection - The act of refusing to accept or consider an idea.

Affirmation

I am free from my fear of rejection, and I know that rejection is a part of the success process. Every time I get rejected, I am that much closer to success.

Are you Scared?

We've all had to face rejection in some way, shape or form. It's how we deal with rejection that separates the winners from the average and the losers. In Business, if you aren't getting rejected, you're not trying. As humans we all have fears, and one of the biggest fears we have is not being good enough. But the good news is that rejection is a part of the success process.

I am an owner of a call center, and I know all about rejection. In sales, it's all about the numbers - it's how many people you can contact within a certain amount of time. I tell my employees if they make hundred calls, they will talk to ten business owners and one will set an appointment. Everyone that I've hired is more than capable of doing the position that I hired them for. The difference between the people who stick around and the people that don't is their disregard of the fear of rejection. Some people will quit because they got cussed out over the phone or someone told them no and got their feelings hurt. Some may not quit, but they will let it ruin their entire day. As humans, we all have emotions and feelings, I get that, but we also can change the way we react to them. You can't let the words of someone you don't even know to affect your production or your life for that matter. Rejection can make or break the best of people, and it can be one of the hardest things to deal with. Even though it's hard, it's something that anyone can learn to control. It's not as hard as not getting what you want out of life.

You only have one life, and if you don't take risks to get ahead, you'll remain right where you are. Some people are afraid to take risks due to fear of rejection. I never had a problem with people failing, I've only had problems with people giving up or quitting. Failure is not a bad thing if we learn from it. Rejection is just a bunch of little lessons that we learn throughout the day. You may not be able to get everyone that you talk to, to do what you want, but if you learn from every failure, from every rejection, you'll become much better, and the percentage of people that you influence will increase significantly. Once you learn how to master the fear of rejection and how to deal with it, you will inherit persistence. Persistence is when you never give up no matter how hard it is. Persistence is when you start to gain momentum, and you become unstoppable. The feeling you get when you get rejected is just temporary. Opportunities are limitless, but you must have a tough skin, to execute and become an effective influencer.

I remember in fifth grade I asked this girl to be my girlfriend, and that day, I happened to have a hole in my shirt, and she said she doesn't go out with people with holes in their clothes. I was upset, and I felt horrible, I knew that if I wanted to win her over, I was going to have to come more decent. From that day on, I was more conscious about what I wore to school. One week later, I decided to try again, and this time I was dressed nice and I brought her a ring to ensure the deal. This time she said yes; we were boyfriend and girlfriend for two weeks, but we later became friends throughout high school. I learned a valuable lesson in that month, no matter how bad it hurt for that brief second, the pain of rejection was only temporary. That was the first time I had to deal with rejection. From that point on, I have been rejected millions of times, but I have never let it get me down. It's not how many times that I've fallen, it's how many times I've gotten up that has got me to where I am now. A lot of people struggle with rejection, but you must remember that there are so many people in this world and not everyone is going to connect with you. It's the people that do connect with you that you should give the attention to, not the people who bring you down. I watched a video on YouTube featuring Grant Cardone and he made dealing with rejection so simple. He said that the only reason people can't deal with rejection is because they don't have enough in their pipeline. That turned on a light switch for me. This goes for anything in life: relationships, sales, money, love, just about anything. If you don't have other things lined up, you're going to feel let down.

Fear is a necessary evil, and if a person is aware of their fears, they are on the right track. As humans, we are programmed to fear, but the fear that we have was created when we were savages, and some of the fears we have programmed in our mind shouldn't be fears to us at all. What I mean by that is through evolution we are no longer hunters, and we don't have to risk our lives to get something to eat for dinner. Some of the fears we have are inborn which means we were born with the fear. Young children fear spiders and snakes before they even know snakes and spiders are poisonous to us. If you try to walk up to a wild bird, most likely that bird will fly away from you, but if you buy a bird at the pet shop, that bird will stand on your finger and trust you with their life. The birds can do this because they unlearned the inborn fear that they have towards humans. As humans, we can do the same thing. We don't have to continue to fear the things that hold us back; we can learn to become like the trained birds and face our fears even if they seem too big for us to handle.

How to Deal with Fear and Rejection

Stop taking everything to heart; you can't take things so personally. Get over it and get back in the field and pursue your dreams.

Write down your fears, and what the worst possible outcome will be. A lot of times, we'll see that the fear that we have isn't that bad.

Prepare and face your fears head on even if you're still scared, just go out and do it, and watch the opportunities come.

Fill up your pipeline; the more options you have, the better chances of success you have. Start thinking in numbers. Every no you get is a no closer to that yes.

Start thinking big, don't let your emotions ruin your goals. If you are an emotional person and you get your feelings hurt easily, you won't last long in sales or business. You must develop a thick skin, and you can't let people's words affect the way you feel.

Don't let your previous call, meeting, presentation, or approach, affect the next one. People can sense your emotions through body language and the tone of your voice.

Never give up because of rejection. You can't fail unless you give up. There is no such thing as failure, only lessons learned. If you are still grinding and learning your craft, you're winning. It may not be tomorrow, it may not be this year, but if you are constantly learning and growing without quitting, you will eventually achieve success.

Use the law of attraction to attract more yeses and fewer no's. Before your meetings, visualize the win in your head in detail, from the presentation all the way through to paperwork. Give people a chance to sell you something; you don't have to buy, just listen.

Know that you're not going to be able to change the minds of everyone, move on to the next lead, and give it all that you have.

Be kind but don't be a pushover. If someone says something out of line, you don't have to agree, but two wrongs don't make a right. Never resort to name calling.

If you are an aggressive person by nature, just walk away and recoup your thoughts before approaching the situation again.

Always follow up no matter what; if they say they have to think about it or they say no. If they say they must think about it, give them a day or two then follow up and close the deal.

Write an email to your customer upon them saying no, stating;

Dear Customer,

I'm sorry we couldn't conduct business today. I feel that I didn't do a good job explaining our products and services to you. My responsibility is to help our customers understand the products and services we provide. I would like to offer you a free consultation at no cost to you; you don't have to buy anything from me, I just want to redeem myself and make sure I explained everything thoroughly. We can meet tomorrow morning, coffee on me.

Your Friend,

YOUR NAME

You may not get a reply to every email you send, but you are letting the customer know that you are serious about what you're selling, and you're relentless. Most people respect that, and you'll boost up your sales tremendously.

Fear and Rejection Quotes

Forget about the consequences of failure. Failure is only a temporary change in direction to set you straight for your next success." – **Denis Waitley**

"Life is not about how much you can hit. It's about how hard you can get hit and keep moving forward. It's about how much you can take and keep moving forward. That's how winning is done." – **Rocky Balboa**

"The greatest barrier to success is the fear of failure." – **Sven Goran Eriksson**

Every experience in your life is being orchestrated to teach you something you need to know to move forward." – **Brian Tracy**

Conclusion

If rejection is your excuse to not bettering yourself, then you need to find a better excuse, rejection isn't hard to accept. Your parents told you no a billion times when you were a kid; you are going to be told no a billion more, suck it up and keep moving forward. Use the law of attraction to attract more yeses. You must follow up on your no's and turn them into yeses. You must face your fears head on even if you're still scared. Control your emotions; don't let a bad experience hinder your future success.

KEY 7 - Prioritize

"The key is not to prioritize what's on your schedule, but to schedule your priorities."

- Stephen Covey

Definition

Priority - When you give more attention to something important before giving attention to something that isn't as important.

Affirmation

I am focusing on the most important things in my life right now. The universe is out to help me succeed, and I am thankful for the life I was given.

What are your priorities?

The other six keys will not work if you do not apply the seventh key and prioritize your goals. What we do with our time is the most important part in becoming successful in sales and business. You are now a professional sales person, and you need to make sure that you are utilizing your day effectively to get maximum results.

What is more important to you and what means the most to you in your life? Is it family, is it security, is it your image, is it freedom, or is it to become the best all-around person you can become? No matter what your goals are in life, you must know that to succeed, you need to be able to prioritize your day from the most important matter to the least important. The most successful people in the world become masters at prioritizing. We have all heard the saying "time is money," and we need to be able to focus our time on the things that will have the most impact on our lives, in a good way, rather than focus on the things that won't. We must be able to sacrifice some of the things we enjoy doing for the greater good. Setting a set schedule is mandatory if you want to become successful in business and sales.

Becoming a successful business person is about creating a good balance and being effective, not just busy. By prioritizing, you become more productive and able to achieve tasks a lot smoother, and you create a clear understanding of what needs to be done. When we don't have priorities, we create delays, unfinished assignments, loss of control, and stress. Stress is the number one cause of businesses failing. Stress from lack of structure, lack of money, or lack of commitment. To be successful in sales, you must learn how to manage your stress. One of the best ways is to create a list of every task you can think of. Identify the urgent tasks and the important tasks. Then decide which task holds the most value to your business, which tasks will make you the most money. If you have conflicting priorities, that hold the same value, finish the one that takes the most amount of time. Then cut out unnecessary tasks that you can live without. When you make a prioritized list, you are making a choice to face the fire and go into war.

We know that no matter what our priorities are, we must make money to get the things we want. So, in business, your number one priority should be sales. We should focus 95% of our time on sales and income and 5% on everything else. Sales should be the number one priority in every business; if it isn't then your business will fail. A business is judged based on the number of products or services sold to the customer. If you aren't selling, then you just have a hobby. Having a hobby is a good place to start, but you can turn that hobby into a business by generating sales and mastering the seven keys. They say that the customer should always come first, and I believe that to be true. If we focus on what the customer wants and deliver it to them, then we can boost our sales. Sales and customers go hand in hand; you can't have sales without people and vice-versa. Therefore, in business, customers and sales should always come first.

Many people make excuses that there is not enough time in the day to accomplish their dreams. Those people are losers, slackers and they make excuses, but not you. You know that priorities are important to your success, and without them, you will be lost. Goals are great, but if you have a prioritized list, kind of like a map to accomplish your most important goals, you have the last key to becoming a success in business and sales. It's the difference in becoming a professional or just dabbling in sales. Think about it like this: you have professional coaches in sports, whose responsibility is to draw out plays to win a game. You are the coach of your own professional career; if you draw out your plays and practice, you will defeat your opponent. The game you are playing is the game of life and your opponent is yourself. The way to win the game of life is to focus on the things that are most important.

I used to be that lazy slacker that had his priorities all mixed up. I was focused on the wrong things because I was out for the quick thrill and not in it for the long run. I would have rather sat at home and smoked pot all day and played video games instead of growing my business. The day that I had my first kid, all my priorities changed. I knew that I had to rethink the way I was living. I knew that to become a great father, I would have to put his needs first. So, the best way I knew how to put him first, was through my own actions and becoming successful in sales and business.

Sometimes we get off track, and that's okay; what's important is getting back on track before it's too late. If we have our priorities written out, we are less likely to fall off, and more likely to learn from the mistakes that we made. Priorities are important because when we face hard times, we can go back to our priorities to see how much it's really affecting our dreams and figure out how much effort we are going to have to put into trying to make it right. A lot of the time, we will find out that the things we stress about aren't going to have any effect on the outcome of our lives. What will have an effect is when you write out your priorities, you will have unlocked the last major key to becoming a successful sales and business person.

How to Prioritize

Write down the 10 things that are most important to you in your life and put them in order from the most important to the least important.

Write out what you do during the day currently, from when you wake up in the morning to when you go to sleep at night.

Then write out how you want your day to look like and include all the 10 priorities into your dream schedule. This is going to be your vision for yourself so remember to dream big, and schedule time for each priority, and spend more time doing the things that are more important to you.

Take your old schedule and rip it up; hang your new schedule up there, somewhere you can see it every day.

If the family is at the top of your list, what about them is important to you. Is it their perception of you, is it their security, or is it their education? You must really dissect your priorities to find out what it is you need to act on to accomplish your goals.

Commit to your priorities. Look at your priorities occasionally (at least three times a year) and keep adding and editing your priorities according to your life situations and commit to making them happen. Your priorities are useless unless you are disciplined enough to work on them consistently.

Priority Quotes

"It is not a daily increase, but a daily decrease. Hack away at the inessentials." - **Bruce Lee**

"Always concentrate on the most valuable use of your time. This is what separates the winners from the losers." - **Brian Tracy**

"Do the hard jobs first. The easy jobs will take care of themselves." - **Dale Carnegie**

"Learn how to separate the majors and the minors. A lot of people don't do well simply because they major in minor things." - **Jim Rohn**

Conclusion

We make time for the things that are most important to us. To really know what is important to us as individuals, we must prioritize our lives from the most important to the least. Making money should be at the top of everyone's list, who are reading this book because money is what drives our businesses. It's what feeds our businesses to grow, and if you want to be successful at business and in sales, your income should come within the top three of your priorities. If we know what we need to do to become the best people we could possibly be, we will work a lot harder to becoming that person. By mastering the last major key and putting your priorities in order, you are solidifying your commitment to become the best business and salesperson you can be.

WORKBOOK

_____

_____

_____

_____

_____

_____

_____

_____

_____

_____

_____

_____

_____

_____

_____
_____
_____
_____
_____
_____
_____
_____
_____
_____
_____
_____
_____
_____
_____
_____
_____
_____
_____
_____
_____
_____
_____
_____
_____

_____

_____

_____

_____

_____

_____

_____

_____

_____

_____

_____

_____

_____

_____

_____

_____

_____

_____

_____

_____

_____

_____

_____

_____

_____

_____

_____

1. CONFIDENCE – Believe in yourself

2. LAW OF ATTRACTION – Think Positive

3. TRUSTWORTHY – Be genuine

4. HUSTLE – Put in the work

5. COMMUNICATE – Share ideas

6. NO FEAR – Be ruthless and relentless

7. PRIORITIZE – What is important to you?

MOMENTUM

In order to gain momentum, you have to get started. Procrastination is one of the most dangerous traits in business. Once you get going, you can't stop. There are no breaks, and the more work you do, the more momentum you will gain. A lot of people ask why they aren't successful, and I can tell you the answer to that is because they quit too early. They either get comfortable or it gets too hard. Whatever you set out to do, don't stop until you've accomplished it. There are too many wishers in this world and not enough doers. They'll say I wish I had that car, I wish I had that house, but they never put an action plan together to get that car or that house. A lot of people have goals, but some are just too low. Set your goals high, if you set your goals high and go after them you'll start to become the person you wish you were.

There are so many perfectionists out there, who are afraid to release a product because it's not perfect. By the time you make it perfect someone else would have already done it, and they would have feedback on how to make it better. Once you have a finished product, share it and sell it to as many people possible. Get feedback from your customers on how to improve it and start gaining momentum. If you wait too long you might be shooting yourself in the foot. This goes for any task, if you have something that needs to be done, write it down and when it's done scratch it off your list. The more you mark down and scratch off the more momentum you'll gain, and when you start to gain momentum, you start to grow. Getting rich isn't hard; it's a long process that will happen once you've paid your dues. Nobody that's gone into business got rich their first day; it took hard work, commitment, desire, and most importantly consistency.

Consistency is one of the best traits in business, if not the best. Someone who is consistent will always become good at whatever they do. We've all heard the saying, practice makes perfect, and while you may not become perfect, you will become better. Consistency is momentums best friend and when you are consistently getting better you become a freight train that can't be stopped. When you gain that kind of momentum, no matter what obstacles stands in your way, you'll be able to knock them out without hesitation. In order to get to that level, you have to become an effective leader, and you have to be able to motivate other people to see your vision.

When everyone else is sleeping you have to be working, when everyone else is watching TV you have to be learning, when everyone else is buying you have to be selling. Be the one who's out of the ordinary. A lot of people feel the need to fit in. Fitting in equals average, and average equals struggle. The people who struggle the most are average or middle class. The rich don't have to worry about money and the poor are taken care of by the government. It's the hard-working middle class that suffers the most, or can suffer the most, because if you lose your job or something happens where you have to dish out a lot of money, you're going to feel it. It takes the same amount of effort to be average that it does to go big, so any chance you have to go big, do it.

The majority of the population in the United States are middle class, in fact eighty percent of America is middle class or average, with an income between twenty to seventy-five thousand dollars a year. About fourteen percent of Americans are poor with an income between zero and twenty thousand dollars a year. Five percent are rich with a yearly income over two hundred thousand a year. Then you have the super rich, these are the people that run the country, they bring in over three hundred thousand dollars a month. Which class do you fall into? Which class do you want to be in? While the middle class is running America, the rich are running the middle class and the super-rich is controlling everything. We have to start thinking differently, instead of reading a book, write a book. The middle class are the consumers, if you want to be rich you have to stop being a consumer and get on the other side and start selling.

Luck is being ready when the right opportunity reaches your doorstep. It's the ones who are ready for anything who get ahead. If you aren't where you want to be, first identify where it is you want to go, turn on your mental GPS and hit the road. Only you have the power to change your outcome of your life.

Create leverage build momentum and stay consistent. Take responsibility for everything that happens in your life and start now. The only thing that is guaranteed in life is death, so do what you can in this lifetime because you won't get another.

Imagine you are at a football game, your favorite team is behind 21 to 28, and the other team is driving the ball down the field. It's fourth and one, and they are on the ten-yard line. The quarterback drops back to pass, and boom, your team intercepts the ball and scores a touchdown. The score is now

28 to 28, and there are only 3 minutes left in the game. Your team is pumped up and ready to kick the onside kick, and you are standing at the edge of your seat biting your fingernails. They kick the ball, and your team recovers the onside kick. Now, your team has a chance to win the game. The quarterback drops back to pass, and the receiver catches the ball and scores a touchdown, as well the extra point. It's now 35 to 28, and your team wins the game. Something magical happened when your team intercepted the ball, the momentum switched, and yours and your teams chance of winning, skyrocketed. Your team was able to carry the momentum to the onside kick recovery, and to the game-winning pass. According to Google, momentum is the driving force gained by the development of a process or course of events. This book will dive deeper into the word momentum, and how to use it to gain prosperity, health, and wealth.

Today, I will do something that my future self will thank me for. I am grateful to have the life that I am living. I have a great career, and I owe it all to God, family, and my determination to better myself. Most people are satisfied with just being mediocre. Most successful people do things in their lives that the majority of the world won't. I dropped out of college after I received an associate's degree to take care of my son and wife; however, my education kept growing. I knew that there was a way to make one hundred thousand dollars plus without a bachelor's degree, and I discovered it at twenty-three years old in sales.

I started reading Think and Grow Rich when I was fifteen years old, and at that time, I didn't really get why my grandfather was making me read it. I just wanted to play football and hang out with my friends. I couldn't really comprehend what the message was. He proceeded to make my first set of affirmations for me and told me to read them every day, twice a day. Again, I did it, but I still didn't know why I was doing it. Eventually, everything that my grandfather wrote down became my reality. I was liked by many, and I always gave my best in everything that I did. I found a company and quickly grew within the company. I was able to travel across the country with my family and build not only a good stable income stream, but also found another world of education. I teamed up with some people in Philadelphia and grew mentally by becoming a student of personal development. I was then laid off, and in return, started my own company.

My first company ended up failing, but I learned from the experience, and I am now growing my business to levels that, 10 years ago, I would have never imagined. I feel like, at the speed that I'm going, I'll be able to retire at thirty-five years old. I don't say that to brag, but to show the world that affirmations do work, personal development does work, and that the universe works with you, not against you, but if you don't put in the time and the effort to do it the right way, you'll stay right where you are. Stay positive, keep focusing on your goals, and live your life to its full potential. Never let anyone tell you that you can't do anything because you can do anything you want to do with your life. No matter what your education, race, or gender is, you have the ability to attract the wealth, health, and the lifestyle you want.

Belief System

Whether it's God, the universe, yourself, or anything else, belief is the starting point. If you believe that that this book will change the way you view life or if you believe that you will pick up a couple new ideas and use them in your daily life I guarantee that this book will help you get to where you want to be. Now before you believe that you will be successful you have to define success.

Success is the progression of a goal that a person reaches by a specific date. Success is different for every person, an example of success is a person that works in their dream job, and everything in their life matches their expectations. They do it because they love it, they know that they may not get rich, but their expectations are met. Once you have your definition of what success is to you, write it down and ask yourself why you want to succeed. What drives you to want to succeed? Why do you wake up in the morning what is your purpose to want to succeed? As a kid I moved back and forth from my mom and my dad, my dad lived in San Diego California and my mom lived in Tucson Arizona.

When I was 6 my mother moved to San Diego so that we would all be in the same town. My mom only stayed for a year and at age 7 my mom left California and went back to Arizona. I lived with my Dad and often visited my grandparents who had a major impact on my life as well. I understood at that point that money was important. I rebelled for a long time, went to a University in Northern California for a year, came back to California then moved to Arizona with a couple of friends. I sold cell phones in San Diego at the mall so as soon as I arrived in Phoenix I applied to work at a couple of cell phone companies there. I got a job, and the pay wasn't too bad for a single guy with roommates. I quickly enrolled into a school for media arts. As I was going to school everyone that went out to Phoenix with me went back to San Diego. I had an obligation and I was going to see it through.

I met my wife while I was selling phones in the mall. We fell in love and from that point on I had my other half. I was 22 years old when we had our first son. I realized that I had an opportunity to give him a better life than I had and everything that I missed out on I could give that to him. At that point in my life I had a why. I also had a belief system. I believed God gave me an opportunity to change my life and create my own destiny. I believed that I could provide for my son because that's what I was put here to do. I also believed in my relationship. I believed that my wife and I were great parents and we could work as a team to give him a great life.

Now that I had a belief system and a why, I was on my way to success. I had a goal to give my son a better life than I had, and I believed that my wife and I could give him that life, but how was this going to work. I quit my job as a cell phone salesman and I was an intern for a music video TV station and going to school full time. My wife worked in the hospital at night and we were barely getting by. One night I got on my knees and prayed that I would get a good job so that I could start helping with the bills. At this time, we were living in a two-bedroom apartment in Arizona, we had our son, and times were hard.

The next morning, I received an email saying they wanted to offer me a job at 14 dollars an hour. I had experience in sales as cell phone salesman from the ages 18 to 21 but I never had an office job where I had to make outbound calls. I worked there for a couple of months and I finally had my how. Now I had my belief system in place my why in place and my how. I was starting to feel good about how my life was turning out. I worked there for four months and by that time I was making 17 an hour and knew that there was more money to be made with this company. The company was expanding, and I wanted to expand too.

The owner hired a lady in Philadelphia and at the last minute she back out. He had everything ready to go for an outside sales agent and no sales agent. I define luck as being prepared when the time comes. Mentally I was ready for a change I had everything in place. My belief system my why and my how were all in effect and I wanted to be what I thought at the time was successful. I went into my boss's office and told him that I wanted the position. He saw in my eyes that I was ready and without hesitation offered me the job. My wife was pregnant with my daughter and I knew I had to make this work, I was going to have two kids at the age of 23 and this job was my meal ticket to provide and give both of my kids a better life than I had. My wife, two kids, and I moved out to Philadelphia and began our journey. I was 23 making six figures, my wife was able to stay at home and I brought in the money. I had my belief system, my why, and my how in place at a young age, and was still in the learning process on how I was going to become truly wealthy.

Get your mind right.

It all starts with your mindset, and how you think. In order to gain momentum, you have to know where you are going. The world makes way for the person who knows where they are heading. Some people have fixed mindsets that they will not allow to be reprogrammed, they are stuck in their ways, and they have the incapability to grow mentally. As children, we were taught to go to school, get the best education, and find a job that will pay just enough to get by, buy a home and retire at 65. Ninety percent of people who attend a four-year university don't even know why they are going to school. Start with why, what motivates you, what drives you to become more than average.

Most of everything we learned in school we do not apply in our daily lives. We have been programmed by the government, the media, and the school system to live a life of meritocracy. That is fine for some people, but obviously, if you are reading this book, you want something better out of your life. Programming your mind is a daily task that shouldn't be taken lightly. If you want success at anything, from sports, business, relationships, or spiritually, it requires practice and goals. Let's take a professional athlete, for example. That a person knows exactly where they want to end up in athletics and they know what it takes to get there.

They have an action plan, whether they know it or not. They work on their craft every day, and every day, they get better. Everyone should apply daily routines to reach their goals. What I have learned is that if you can trick your mind into believing something that is not yet true or real, it will eventually turn into your reality.

One activity that has worked for me repeatedly is affirmations. Anyone who has worked for me has had to write out their affirmations before they even start training. Affirmations, as I define it to my employees, are putting your goals into present tense. To affirm something means to state as a fact, it is a pledge, a vow, a proclamation. The key to making your affirmations work is to read them to yourself every single day and believe them.

If you are a gym rat, you probably don't feel right if you skip the gym because it becomes a habit. If you are as serious about the quality of your life, as you are about the gym life, not only will you reach your physical goals, but you will have a better chance of succeeding in every aspect of your life. When writing out your affirmations, make sure you are including financial goals, physical goals, spiritual goals, relationship goals, and family goals along with any other goals that you can think of that will make you happy.

We have to think of ourselves as a company, and the jobs that we have are just our clients. Your 9 to 5 is your biggest client. How do you grow your company? You establish more income streams. There are so many things out there that you can do to make extra money, and with the ease of having the world at your fingertips, the opportunities are limitless. If the mind can conceive it, then the mind can achieve it. The only thing that is holding you back are the excuses that you are making. When you get off of work, what do you do? Most people just get in their car and listen to music that is irrelevant to their lives.

Once they get home, they spend 3 hours in front of a TV that's not helping them reach their goals.

People wonder why their lives are the way they are, and I ask them what they do in their free time, and most people can't even tell me. Things like Facebook and Instagram are taking over people's lives, and it's kind of sad. I can barely have a conversation with someone without them looking at their cell phones at least once. If you want to be a millionaire, use social networking to better yourself and promote your business. Write out a list of ten goals, circle the goal that you think you can achieve the fastest, and write down seven action steps that will help you achieve that goal.

Repeat the steps until all of your goals are met, then start over with another list of 10 goals. Ensure you are using the SMART goal setting system, making sure that your goal is specific, measurable, attainable, relevant, and most importantly time bound. Next, write down 12 reasons why you will succeed. Then make your affirmations, which means putting your goals into present tense. The key to making these affirmations work is looking in the mirror directly into your own eyes; you can't lie to yourself. Say them twice a day, once when you wake up in the morning and once before you go to bed at night. In order to do something you've never done, you have to become the person you've never been. So, the biggest part is discipline. If you can discipline yourself to do this every day, you'll land right on the head of success.

Create an action plan.

Once you have your why and affirmations written out, it's time to put your plan into action. Knowledge is not power applied; knowledge is power. The only way to make your dreams come true is to work for them. No one will take action for you; this is something that only you can do. Take each one of your affirmations and dissect them. Let's say that one of your affirmations is to buy your first home, what action steps do you have to take to get there? How much money are you going to need for a down payment, what will your credit scores have to be, how much income will you need monthly to pay the mortgage? Now, break those down even more. Let's say you need ten thousand dollars down and you make three thousand a month, your total monthly cost of living is two thousand five hundred. You have five hundred dollars that you can put away every month, in an account that you don't use often, separated from all your other monies. It will take you about a year in a half to have your down payment. If you incur extra money, put that money into that account, but stick to your guns and keep paying yourself five hundred dollars every month. This will take a lot of discipline, consistency, and sacrifice. You may have to give up that vacation that you were planning for the past five years; you might have to give up some extracurricular activities.

The question you have to ask yourself is, are your goals more important to you than your comfort? If it is, then it will show in the end result. You can't let anything or anyone stand in your way of accomplishing your goal. Do the math to verify and break it down into yearly, monthly, and daily tasks that will help you accomplish those goals. Over time, your action plan may change, but the one thing that has to be consistent is you. Without action, we cannot generate momentum, and momentum is the driving force gained by the development of the process. If you follow this process and take action, you will be a step closer to your dreams.

Controlling our Emotions

Over time, you are going to have some difficulties. In order to stay consistent, you have to keep working on your affirmations. You have to create good habits, and you can't let others bring you down. I see it all the time; people let their emotions and feelings take control of their logical thinking. The only person who really cares if you're upset is you. It's all a mindset, and if you feel a certain way, you are the only one who feels the emotion. I understand that as humans, we all have feelings that affect our daily lives, but who really cares. We each have control over our minds and control the way we feel.

Once you're able to set your emotions aside and start thinking rationally and logically, you will grow, and in turn, you will make more money and live a happy life. It's one of the hardest things to overcome because we are programmed to feel a certain way when another person offends you or does something to hurt you. In sales, it also makes it harder if you're running off of emotion. If you get cussed out at one door or on one phone, call and take that frustration to the next customer, he'll be able to feel the vibe that you carried from that last client who got you all frazzled. If we can learn to make that feeling go away, we will be able to get through the day a lot smoother, and we'll be able to make more money, as well as live a life of fulfillment. In an office setting, the worst thing about negative energy is that it's contagious and will rub off on those around you. Not only is that person making themselves stressed out, but they are also making everyone who comes in contact with them feel uncomfortable.

According to an article on worksmartlivesmart.com, we have to understand what that person is expecting to gain by being so difficult. Does that person think that they aren't being listened to or aren't important? Once we figure out what the person expects to gain by being difficult, we can start to diagnose the problem and fix it. As a team leader, we have to make sure that our team is all on the same page and make sure that there is an overall team goal that we all are working towards. Negative energy is a business killer, and if it cannot be fixed, cut the bad apple from the tree so the disease doesn't spread, and the company isn't burning leads.

Employees may not like each other, but they have to learn to work together if they both want to reach their goals of becoming successful. If you are on the other end and you feel uncomfortable because you don't like someone in your office, get over it and work together or if there are no means to an end and you are truly unhappy, then find another office that will complete your satisfaction as an employee. The first thing is to try to squash it and move forward. If you have a disgruntled client, take a quick five minutes break, reflect on your reason for being there, use pictures of kids, read your affirmations, think of being happy and control your mind. Get in the habit of thinking happy thoughts. Thoughts lead to feelings, and if you can control your thoughts, you can control your feelings. Make today better than yesterday and don't let other people control the way you feel.

Managing Relationships

There are so many different types of people in this world and not everyone is going to get along. Relationships don't have to be intimate, you can have business associates, friends, and family. Each different type of relationship requires different levels of attention. The more attention you give, the more that relationship will grow.

A business relationship is somewhat like a marriage, and the business is the child. If both partners aren't on the same page, the business will fail. Both partners must have the same agenda, and if one partner is putting in more work than the other, eventually the partner who is putting in the work will get fed up and the partnership will split. You must be very careful when you decide to make a business partner. If you're not sure if that person will make a good partner don't get into business with them.

You become the median of the five people you hang around most. If you are hanging around five losers, you'll probably end up a loser. If you hang around five successful people, your chance of becoming a success is one hundred times more likely. Find a mentor or someone that has what you want out of life and study that person. Be careful who you allow in your circle, they can either bring you down or lift you up.

Family plays a very important role when it comes to business. The influence that a family member has, can detour you from seeing your full potential. It's up to you to make the decision to go into business for yourself not theirs. What worked for them may not work for you, and what works for you may not work for them. Most of the time family members have good intentions, they don't want you to fail or get hurt, so they tell you your idea is crazy, and you just need to get a steady job. It's not their fault, they are just giving you advice from their perspective. They bring their fears to you because they feel that they can't do it.

In your heart, if you know that going into business is the right choice for you, then do it. If you have a family that supports your decision, it's like having a train push you forward until you reach success, momentum. Not all family members are blood-related. Over the years I've made friends that I consider family, and sometimes those friends get jealous and try to tell you things that might jeopardize your chance of success.

Finding a significant other that is right for you can seem like something that will never happen, but it will. Once you've found that right person communication is the key to making it work. In my marriage we have been through our ups and downs but it's communication that always brings us back together. What I mean by that I, is both sides have to be able to hear each other out. For example my wife and I were separated for some time due to lack of communication, I felt like she was bored of me and I shut down, when I shut down she shut down and we separated.

When we both started talking again we talked about what was bothering us and we worked it out. It sounds simple, but not when emotions come into play and our hearts take over. Emotions can lead us to do some pretty stupid things if we don't think about what we are doing before we do it. The two greatest powers in this world are fear and love and when you mix the two it's like a chemical explosion in our heads. Before saying something that you will regret later, take a quick break and get some alone time to cool off. Always compromise, if you find the right person you have to look at things from their point of view. If you have to make a decision together try to meet in the middle, don't be demanding.

A relationship is like a living organism, if you don't take the time to feed it and care for it, it will die. Both sides have to have the will to want to make it work, if both sides don't, it's up to the one who does to try to spark that flame back up. If that's not possible, it's okay to move on. If you have two people who both want success in all aspects of life then I call those power couples, and they will be able to take down any challenges that come their way.

Some relationships are toxic and shouldn't be tried to work out. If you think you are in one of those relationships, take a break. See if you feel better without that person in your life. If they are right for you, they will find their way back. It's okay to move on sometimes and it may feel like the end of the world, but I promise you that it's not.

Both people in the relationship have to be on the same page of what they want out of life. If one person wants to have a family and the other one can't stand kids, someone isn't going to get all they want out of their life. How much does a person have to love another person to give up on what they really want out of life? That question I will leave for you to answer.

Creating Habits

According to Maxwell Malts, a world-renowned plastic surgeon in the 1950s, it takes a person 21 days to form a new habit. He found this out when he performed surgery on his patients. It took them around 21 days to get used to their new face, and his results would follow behind him, and they would be used to help people in personal development for decades. More studies were done over the years and come to find out it takes longer than 21 days. For most people, it will take around two months to actually form a habit.

The definition of a habit, according to Wikipedia, is a routine of behavior that is regularly repeated and tends to occur unconsciously. What is the key to forming a habit? I believe that it is commitment and dedication that gets the job done, and most people lack in those traits; however, most people aren't reading this book either. The best way to form a habit is to write down what you want to accomplish and place it in your daily goal list and mark it down once it's accomplished. When you cross it off, you will feel a sense of accomplishment, which will release endorphins and make you happy. Do this for two months every day, and you will start to form the habits. One of the first personal development books I read was Steven Covey's 7 Habits of highly effective people, and in the book, he explains how to develop a habit and the processes in which it takes to make the habits stick. The 7 traits were; be goal-oriented, be result-oriented, be action-oriented, be people oriented, be health-oriented, stay honest, and be self-disciplined.

I will touch on each habit, but I recommend that you also buy the book for more detail. We touched on being goal-oriented a little bit already, and I believe this is the most useful habit. Not many people follow through with their goals, and most people don't even set goals. Write down your goals, and you'll already be ahead of 90% of Americans. The second is result-orientated. The way to do that is through continuous practice and concentrate on one thing at a time until it is accomplished. The third is action-orientated, which can be accomplished by getting the job done fast. A good read for this habit is The Power of Now by Eckhart Tolle. By putting your fears to the side and giving 100% towards your most important goal and getting it done promptly, you will become action-oriented.

The fourth is being people-oriented. In order to be successful, you must have people skills. Not everyone was born with people skills, but everyone can learn how to get along with others and make people like them. A good read on this Habit is Dale Carnegies' How to win friends and influence people. Basically, the key to being people-oriented is being kind, having patience, and being understanding. The fifth habit is being health-oriented, by eating healthy, working out, and making sure that your body and mind are both strong in every way. Get a gym membership and start monitoring what you eat. The sixth habit is staying honest. This means having integrity and values in your life. Be truthful to other people, but most of all, be truthful to yourself. You never adjust your morals, integrity, or values for anything or anyone. Stand up for what you believe in and believe in what you stand for. The last habit is being self-disciplined. Being self-disciplined will assure you succeeding in the other six habits. Be your worst critic, make sure you're not too hard on yourself though, never let anything that is out of your control affect your attitude. Developing good habits will help you grow to your full potential, so remember to be persistent, see yourself already developing the habit, and stick to your script of becoming the best person you can be.

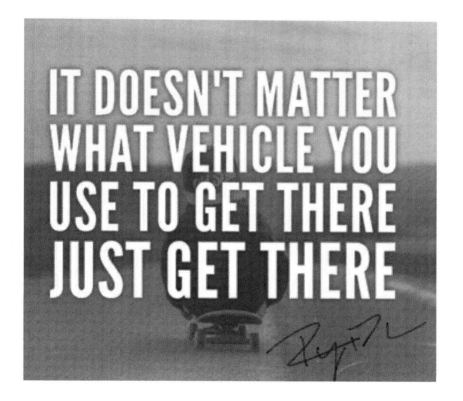

Leadership

Lead from the front, lead to win. Leaders have to be able to make a decision, and be willing to do it themselves. A good leader has to be a people person, and must be able to persuade others to their way of thinking. A good leader must show a genuine interest in helping other people, and has the ability to listen and but also be stern in what they expect out of their team. It's the small things that leaders do, that make them great leaders. There are many levels of leadership, in the business world. You have managers, general managers, regional managers, vice presidents, presidents, chief executive officer, etcetera. Each time you move up in levels of management your pay will increase, because of the level of responsibility or conflict you take on.

Leaders get paid for solving problems and to motivate their team to reach their full potential, they equip their team with the resources necessary for success. A leader is willing to go where no one has gone before and clear a path for others to follow. Leaders must be fearless and be willing to make sacrifices, when no one else was. If we look back at history, great leaders have always possessed these qualities. Let's take a look at Abraham Lincoln, he was liked and respected by many, but not by everyone, because of his views on slavery. He wanted slavery to end, and he wanted to be the leader to do so. He knew the risks of doing so, but he was fearless and courageous in his actions. In 1860 he ran against Steven Douglas and won the presidency. On April 12th, 1861 the Confederacy fired on Fort Sumter and began the deadliest war in America. On January 1st, 1863 Lincoln issued the emancipation proclamation which ended slavery in America. In 1864 Lincoln ran again, and easily won the election.

On April 14th, 1865 John Wilkes Booth shot Lincoln to death. Lincoln was willing to die for what he believed in, and by doing so he led a whole nation to become the country we are today, full of different ethnicities from all over the world. People come to America because they have a dream and we owe that to Lincoln, because without his courage and leadership people of color would not have the opportunities that we have today. There were many other great leaders in this country that we can look into, too many to mention, but here are a few to study; Martin Luther King, Henry Ford, Steve Jobs, Eleanor Roosevelt, and John F. Kennedy.

The best leadership books that I have read have been from John C Maxwell, a pastor, author, and speaker who is an expert on leadership. His take on leadership is, it has five levels. One is being a positional leader, which is based on the title of the position, like a manager or a supervisor. If someone has to follow you because they have to, and they don't want to, you'll get the least amount of effort. The second level is the permission level, which means people are following you because they want to. They like you and they want to work for you. A permission level leader will listen, observe, learn, and know how to serve others.

Level number three is the production level, which means they lead by example. They show leadership by action and production, and are the model for what to do. At level number three you begin to gain momentum and it becomes easy to lead. Level number four is the people development level, which means they equip their team to grow and develop into a top producer and a better person. They place the right people in the right positions, and they recruit the right people. At the people development level you have to be able to teach others how to teach others. The last step is the pinnacle level, at this level they follow you because they respect you, what you have accomplished, and what you represent.

The five levels of leadership are a great gage to see what kind of leader you are and what you need to do to become a level five leader. If you are a level two leader, you have to become a level three leader before moving on to level four and five. Leadership can be learned just like any other skill trade. You have to learn and practice these qualities to become a great effective leader. Keep learning and growing, and remember to learn to teach and put into action, don't just learn to learn.

Income

Everyone wants to be the best at what they do, but not everyone is willing to take the risk. Why do some people take risks and others don't? What is the difference between the two types of people? The answer is simple; a lot of people just don't want to leave their comfort zones because they fear what they don't know. Fear is something that is necessary to have as human beings because, without it, we would probably no longer exist on this planet. However, in business, in order to get ahead, we have to take risks. We have to reprogram our brains to think that if we take a risk, the end result will hurt us.

We have to leave our comfort zones and do something out of the ordinary to become better. We have to weigh the risk versus reward, and the best way to do that is the old fashion pros and cons list. Ninety percent of the time the pros will outweigh the cons, and you will see that you should take that leap of faith. The one thing that holds us back is the unknown factor. What will happen if I take this leap of faith and it doesn't work out? A better question should be what will happen if I don't take this leap of faith?

The answer to the second question is an easy one; everything will stay exactly the same. In order to make a change, we have to change the way we think and take more risks. Don't be stupid and start taking risks without weighing out the outcome. Make sure that before you make any big decisions that you map it out and weigh the pros and cons. In an article written in Forbes magazine called The Greatest Risks They Ever took by Katy Finneran, she quoted Ronald Heifetz, a

Harvard University Professor "Successful people are those who don't become disheartened and try again." Indeed, a successful person is persistent, but most of all, a successful person is fearless, always taking risks repeatedly until it eventually pays off.

I believe that anyone that wants to be a millionaire should be a part of some MLM group. It cost a little bit of money to join, but the outcome is much greater. You will surround yourself with positive people, and you might make an extra couple of dollars on accident. Invest in yourself by buying personal development books, listening to audio, and watching movies and TV shows that are inspiring and not just entertaining.

You won't save your way to a million dollars, so the answer to becoming a millionaire is to make more money. Make your money work for you. Start from the bottom and work your way up to the top; every self-made millionaire started in the same position you're in right now. In sales, it's easy to make your money work for you, especially if you are an independent agent. If your commission is 20% of the sale, hire five people, give them 15%, and train them to do the work for you; that's called leverage. Invest in long-term stocks and set a date to take it out in 10 years, make sure the stocks you buy pay out dividends. Do not touch that money until the date you specified. Don't spend all of your money on material things like fancy clothes, expensive cars, boats, and other unnecessary things. Monitor your money, look at it every day and watch it grow. An average millionaire makes a salary of around two hundred thousand a year, but has their money working for them in other places. In order to make this work, you have to be persistent.

Persistence

We have all had times where we have given up on something, or just quit because something was too hard, or it didn't work out the first time. A lot of people will start something new, try it out, and just give up. This is fine if you're just exploring different opportunities and hobbies, but if you are trying to actually be good at it, if it's something that you truly want to be successful in and you know that it will eventually get you to the lifestyle you want to live, why would you give up? People usually give up right before they are about to reach the place that will put them in the position they want to be. If you ever read the book Think and Grow Rich, you should remember the story of the man who gave up too soon, and what happened when he sold his land, and the next guy came in and worked for a short period of time and made a fortune.

In a conversation with my grandfather, he told me that his goal was to be the first black head coach in the NFL and reach 20 million dollars. Even though my grandfather was still successful, he said the reason he didn't reach his goals was that he gave up after 17 years as an assistant coach, because of politics. He was able to see other opportunities that he wanted to explore, such as radio stations and car dealerships, and he was able to learn those businesses and become successful in those industries, but he never reached that 20 million. I heard a sense of regret in his voice when he told me that, so I took it to heart and decided that no matter how long I've been in my industry, and no matter how hard times get, I will continue on my mission until I reach my goals.

How do we stay persistent and use failure as a tool to become better? It starts with how we view the world if we think that the world is out to harm us and everything is just sort of a conspiracy theory, that's exactly what it will be. If we believe that the world is out to help us and that everything happens for a reason, we are able to learn from our mistakes or our misfortunes and become stronger, wiser, and more likely to succeed the next time around. We have to fail forward, which means we have to learn from our failures in order to grow.

We have to be willing to take risks, and if you are a salesperson or a business owner, I understand that you know this to be true. I believe that this is, if not the most important key to success, the second most important key after goal setting. If you turn your tasks into habits, eventually, you will become one of the best at whatever it is that you do. Most people change their careers so many times that they never get to the position that they started out for.

Do you think that people who try new things every year are benefiting more than those who have mastered one? Is persistence more important than goal setting? How do we know when to call it quits?

Work Smarter or Harder?

We've all heard the saying, "work smarter, not harder." To me, this seems to be a false statement. Without hard work, how can we get the opportunity to work smart? Everyone has to start somewhere, and without that boost of hard work, we won't be able to get the chance to use our mind to excel. I believe that hard work does pay off; however, we should work even smarter to ensure our success. Most people just work hard continuously until the day they pass away, never getting the chance to explore all of their true potentials.

Why does this happen, why do most people just settle for the standard? Again, it's all a mindset; most people think the same way, brainwashed by the media and the public, most people believe that hard work always pays off; most people just don't get it. Nobody thinks the exact same way, but once our mind is opened up to explore what life really has to offer, we can grow and expand. For years, I was selfish not sharing my knowledge with others, thinking that I would benefit from being secretive, not knowing that if I spread my knowledge, I can double, triple, quadruple, my income. I thought that if I put in the hard work that I would reach my goals, I was getting by, but not reaching my full potential.

After eight years of hard work and obtaining knowledge, I am applying the knowledge and now working smart. Anyone who has been successful at anything will tell you that it does take a lot of hard work to succeed. Anyone who is successful and stays successful will tell you that you have to work smart in order to sustain the success.

Journey to success

 This part of the book is about my experiences that occurred in my life, which led me to become my own boss. It will have stories about how I started from the bottom and made my way to the top, and still climbing. I will take you through my daily tasks that I do now; the things I did wrong and the things I did right. It will mention my mentors and give credit to all that have helped me on my way. I will start my story with my very first job; well, it wasn't really a job, it was more like chores in a work environment.

When I was about nine years old, my grandfather owned a dealership in Hayward, California, and my father was the customer service manager. I would go to work with my dad, and he would give me assignments, like sweeping, taking out the trash, or load up the vending machines. My favorite was always loading the vending machine because I would always get a free soda and a snack. I loved going into work with my dad; I always dressed up in slacks, a button up with a tie, and a blazer with nice shiny shoes.

It made me feel good walking through the dealership looking nice, everyone was always so friendly, always smiling and waving. I would stop and talk to them; I made a lot of friends, but the people who always stood out to me were the sales guys out in the lot. I loved cars, so I was always in the lot. I would always get in the cars and pretend that I was driving them; my favorite car to sit in was the convertible Camaro and the year was 1995.

I would watch the sales guys talk to the customers and watched how they interacted with them. I studied them and watched how they moved and how they talked. I remember how friendly they were to the customers. They always seemed like they knew the people they were talking to. Even though I didn't get paid for the time that I spent at the dealership, it taught me responsibility, hard work, and most of all how to dress sharp. My grandfather ended up selling the dealership in Hayward and buying a dealership in Los Angeles, and I moved back to San Diego.

My first experience in a work environment was awesome, but it wasn't until I was 17 that I had my next job, which actually paid me in real money. While going to high school, my father wouldn't let me get a job; he said my job was to be a student and an athlete. I enjoyed playing sports like baseball, basketball, and my favorite of all time, football. Football has always been a part of my life from the day I was born until now. To some people, football is just a game, but to me, football was and is still a lifestyle, and it played a huge role in how I handle my life and run my businesses today.

Football taught me how to compete, how to give it all that I have; it taught me that, in life, you aren't always going to win, and most of all how to be a team player. My senior year in high school, I was the quarterback, and I led my team to a CIF championship, which we lost, and I still feel the pain today of my final high school game in QUALCOMM stadium; the score was 20-3. I use that pain today to always try to be the number one because I did not enjoy being runner-up.

Just a little background on how football has had an impact on my life. My father, Allan Durden, who was an all-American football player at the University of Arizona met my mother, Julie Olson, while in college. I was born January 11, 1986, in Tucson Arizona. My very first memory I have is on the football field with my dad; I don't remember how old I was, maybe two or three, but I remember how big it looked and it just felt like home. My grandfather was the running back coach for the San Diego Chargers for 17 years.

My father was drafted in 1986 by the Detroit Lions, the same year that I was born. My mother and I struggled; she didn't have a car, so we had to ride the bus everywhere. She didn't have a lot of money, so when I was six years old, my mom and I moved from Tucson Arizona to San Diego CA. My father was already living there at the time, and he was no longer playing football due to an injury. I remember going back and forth to my moms and dads, and I enjoyed it. I wasn't used to my parents living in the same state. One day, when I was about seven or eight years old, my mother moved back to Tucson because it was so expensive to live there, and it was just my dad and I living in San Diego.

A year or two later, my father met my stepmother, Angela Williams, and they had a little girl, Alexis Ryan Williams Durden, my sister. This was at the same time my grandfather had the dealership in Hayward, CA. When she was born, everyone loved her, but no one as much as me. I was so excited to be a big brother, I was the only child for ten years, and now, I have someone I can play with and look after. I have always been protective of my baby sister and made sure that she was always okay. She taught me how to be responsible for another human being other than myself.

My childhood consisted of sports school and playing outside with my friends. I can't say that we were rich, but we got by, and sometimes, times were hard, but my father always made sure we had everything we needed. I got a lot of my work ethic from my father, but I didn't take the same route. I wanted to own my business, and he wanted to earn a prestigious position at a major corporation. I didn't like the rules and regulations that you had to follow in the corporate world. I wanted the freedom to do anything I wanted to do. I was a rebel, and I wanted to create my own path.

FIRST DAYS OF EMPLOYMENT

After the football season during my senior year, my father finally lets me get a job, working for him at a motorcycle shop. He was the customer service manager there as well. I was in charge of cleaning up the lot, picking up and dropping off motorcycles, putting seat covers on dirt bikes, mounting tires, and again, the vending machines from my grandfather's dealership somehow made their way into the motorcycle shop. Yes, the same exact ones.

Now, when I was filling up the vending machine, there were always like two or three guys waiting for me to give them a free candy bar and a can of soda. I could have gotten in trouble, but I still hooked up with my friends in the shop. I did work hard, but like any other teenager, I goofed off and slacked from time to time. I remember one day this guy came down the stairs with five beautiful girls. I asked him what he did, and he said media. At that time, I thought that was the coolest thing in the world, what a seventeen-year-old boy wouldn't think was cool. That day, I made a choice that I wanted to do something in media, marketing, or sales.

Not only was he with girls, but he also didn't dress up in a suit and tie like the other guys. He had his own office on the top floor, and it looked like he just came and went as he pleased. Like I mentioned before, I was a teenager, and I did some pretty foolish things, but nothing as foolish as what I was about to do, which lead to me being terminated by my own father. I was in the back one day driving the forklift, this forklift had gears, and I would always switch the gears to go faster. We were in a motorcycle shop, surrounded by speed, and I enjoyed going fast. I turned a corner, shifted up, and the forklift flipped. I ran underneath the forklift almost getting pummeled by the forks. I just stood there in disbelief.

About thirty seconds later, my dad came out with a look of disgust on his face, "get the truck and go home," I could remember how angry he sounded. That night, we didn't speak about it; it was something that we never discussed again. That was my first job; it was fun while it lasted, and I got paid real money for the first time. My paychecks were about seven hundred dollars every two weeks, and I didn't have any bills, so I enjoyed having little money. Shortly after I was fired, I moved out of my Dad's house to go live with one of my friends, and I lived in his garage. I was seventeen years old and still in high school.

I didn't have a job, so I started selling weed for extra money. Even though I was selling weed out of my friend's garage, I still went to school and graduated with a 3.2 GPA. I graduated high school in 2004, and shortly after, I moved up to Turlock, CA, to attend California State Stanislaus for one semester. I really didn't want to leave San Diego; I had a girlfriend, and that school didn't have a football team. When I got out there, I got a job at a variety store across the street from the campus. I networked and met people who were in the weed business and started selling weed out of the variety store.

My friends would show up, and we would drink beers in the cooler while I was working. I had no sense of the consequences I was about to suffer. One day, I was sitting on my balcony smoking a joint with a friend, and a resident advisor walk by. We said good morning, and I thought everything was fine. My friend and I were leaving the dorms to go pick up another friend from work, and two police officers greeted us at the front gate. The resident advisor was standing right there with them.

I had the weed in my pocket, and they brought me in, weighed the weed, and gave me a court date. I ended up only having to pay a ticket, but they kicked me out of the dorms. I did not complete one single class; I was living in the dorms partying every single day, just taking advantage of living for free off of my father's money and I had extra money to spend on partying, as well as doing things I probably shouldn't have been doing, and now I had nowhere to live. During Christmas vacation, I ended up getting into trouble with the law again.

My friends and I were at a party, and I borrowed my friend's car to go to the store. I had a beer in my lap, and I was really drunk, so I was scared and super stupid. While I was driving back to the party, I saw flashing lights behind me, and I just sped off. I had no idea where I was, and I had no sense of direction. I just put the pedal to the metal and tried to get away as fast as I could. I ended up running into a light pole, jumped out on foot, ran, and got away from the police.

I walked around the neighborhood for about two hours, and finally, I saw some kids from the party. There were about four of them; they jumped out of the car and started to rush me throwing punches, saying, "The cops said we can beat you up." I told them to just take me to jail, and that's just what they did. I ended up only doing three months in county jail for a second DUI. When I got out, I moved back to San Diego. I really didn't know what I was going to do with my life; I was lost.

I missed football and wanted to play, but I was also rebelling at the time and just wanted to hang out with my friends and get drunk and high all day. I was depressed from a breakup with my girlfriend, and I lost sight of my goals and dreams. I always dreamed of playing football. I had a vision in my head of how my life was supposed to be, and it wasn't like that at all. I didn't know what to do; I just knew that I had to do better. I had to get out of this funk I had to try, I was wasting my life away, getting in trouble with the law, not motivated, just young and dumb. I went and applied for a cell phone sales job at the mall in San Diego. My first interview was in the mall cafeteria, with an Asian guy who looked sharp and spoke very well.

He asked if I had any sales experience, I said no, but I know I'll be good at it. He took off his watch and said, "Sell this to me." I didn't know what to say. I just started talking. I realized at that moment that I really didn't know how to sell, but it seemed like I could bull shit my way through it and make some money. I ended up getting the job and attended some really great training courses with the company. I enjoyed talking to people, and most of all, I liked getting paid for my efforts. I ended up working in the cell phone industry for four years, jumping from mall to mall in San Diego and Phoenix.

I was excelling in the cell phone business, was a manager at a kiosk, and I was in charge of 5 employees. I saw how fast I moved up, and the money was okay, but I couldn't see myself in malls all my life. During the time I was working in the cell phone business, I decided to give school another shot. I ended up moving out to Phoenix with some friends, and I saw a commercial on the TV advertising a degree in Media Arts. I remembered the guy at the motorcycle shop and how he had all those girls around him, and how cool he looked.

I immediately called my dad and told him I wanted to enroll back into school. The vision in my head was me surrounded by beautiful women and getting paid for it. I graduated from that college with an associate degree in media arts, and when I went to transfer my credits to another school, none of my credits was transferred. I was devastated, when I first started going to school there; I specifically asked if I could transfer my credits to any university and they said yes. I was bamboozled, they weren't accredited, and now I had a bad taste in the mouth for schools.

I was now in debt of $60,000.00 and not only that, what was I going to do with an Associate's Degree in media arts? I started an internship with a local Television station that played music videos 24 hours a day, I organized the film, made the transitions from one video to another, and I put the subtitles at the bottom with the artist name, song title, record label, and the video director's name. I also did some teasers and short fifteen-second commercials for the station, they called them bumpers.

One day, I went to my internship, and the owner's girlfriend was in the station going absolutely nuts. There was one other intern, and she used to pick me up and give me rides to the station. We both kept knocking at the door; the owner's girlfriend came out and started yelling at us to go away. We thought she was on some kind of drug, so we called the owner, and he wasn't answering the phone. I never showed back up to that internship, and I felt like I wasted two months of my life for some crazy people. I did learn a thing or two while I was there, and it's not like I was getting paid to do the work anyways, so I was done.

After that incident, I started my own production company and hired a couple of friends. We did music videos, commercials, and a lot of live shows for all kinds of artists of all different genres. The vision I had in my head of me being surrounded by a bunch of women and getting paid for it came to reality. I was constantly behind my camera, and the things that the girls did in front of the camera are another story for another book. Business was good; I was working as a cell phone salesperson during the day and a video producer at night.

I made enough money to provide for me, but my new girlfriend, Annette, who later on became my wife, was pregnant, and I knew I had to do something different. The nightlife, going out with local rock stars and rap groups, was getting old; I partied way too much, and I knew that if I continued down that path, I would create my own demise. I saw quickly that the life I was chasing wasn't really the life I wanted to live. I was pursuing the wrong dream, and I needed to make a change.

I applied for a couple of positions and ended up getting hired at a water company selling water door to door. It was a fun job, and they pay us salary plus commission, but I couldn't really see myself selling water all my life, so that only lasted a couple of months. Luckily, I did quit because, a couple of months later, the company fired everyone and sold the company. I would have been out of a job anyway.

I was never really big on religion, but I remember one night in our little apartment in north Phoenix, getting on my knees and praying to God for an opportunity to provide for my new family. I didn't know it at the time, but this was the first time that I used the "secret" to benefit me financially. In my heart, I really believed that God was going to point me in the right direction and give me an opportunity, and I was right. The next day, my prayers were answered; I got a call from a company asking me to come in for an interview and the starting pay was $14.00 plus commission.

The pay was around the same as the water company, but I didn't have to walk in the hot sun knocking on doors. I had my own desk, my own computer, and my own extension. I figured I could reach a whole lot more people from the phone than I was walking around from house to house. I was so excited to start my new job, I had a positive attitude, and I was ready for anything life had to throw my way.

The Payment Industry

In 2007, I had my first kid, Isaiah Kevin Durden. This is when I started gaining my momentum. Becoming a father changed my life completely. I had a purpose that was bigger than me. I had to make money to provide for the three of us and life was getting serious, so I got serious. The company I worked for did credit card processing, and my responsibilities were to call business owners and set appointments for senior reps to meet with them and sign them up.

I studied and took the job very seriously, and within four months, I was given the opportunity to go out to Philadelphia to be a senior rep and make over one hundred thousand dollars a year. I jumped on that opportunity so fast, and I put my nose into the books; I studied day in and day out until I knew it as if I wrote it. I owned the script and the rebuttals, I made flash cards, recordings, hung the script up in my shower, made videos, anything that I could to become the best at it.

In 2008, at the same time, I was moving to Philadelphia, my girlfriend and I had another baby, Alyiah Ann Durden. I knew that I had to make this work; I didn't want to be a failure and let my growing family down. I ended up making one hundred and twenty thousand dollars that year, and I was twenty-two years old. It's not a whole lot of money, but for a twenty-two-year-old, it made me feel pretty good about myself. While I was driving in my car from appointment to appointment, I turned my car into Drive Time University.

I started listening to personal development CDs, and I tried to only focus my energy on things that were going to help me succeed in my line of work. I enjoyed learning about the human mind and how to control it. One of the first books I read, which was given to me by my grandfather when I was 15, was Think and Grow Rich by Napoleon Hill. He actually made my first set of affirmations for me and suggested that I read them every night. I did for the most part, and I believe that later on in my life, they came back to help me.

How I explain affirmations is basically putting your goals into present tense; for example, writing down a goal, such as I will make one hundred thousand dollars this year or I am in the best shape of my life and taking vacations all over the world. Whatever your goals are, write them down in the present tense and say them every night, and believe that they have already happened, and they will. I've written two sets of affirmations on my own, and most of what I have written down has come true. I'm still working on my second set of affirmations.

It's been about four years, but I know that they will happen eventually. Just thinking about your goals isn't enough. You have to see them, say them, memorize them, and make them a part of your everyday life. I learned a lot driving around, but nothing better than goal setting. Goal setting is the number-one key to success. If you have no path to follow, you will get lost. I was in love with what I did; I saved people's money, and I made a lot of it.

I used what I learned in my car every day to help these business owners save money on their overall business expenses. The first chapter of Think and Grow Rich was Desire, and I had a burning desire to succeed. I wanted to give my family the best life possible. I didn't know it at the time, but listening to those CDs in my car was the best thing I could have done. Every obstacle that stood in my way, I was able to either avoid or bounce back so fast that it seemed like it never happened.

I started network marketing, to make a little extra money and to get around positive people. I followed the roadmap that the company laid out, and my wife and I started making a pretty penny off of the product, which was selling legal insurance. I enjoyed network marketing because of the positive energy that was spread throughout the building. Everyone was always so optimistic about life, and it made me optimistic about everything that I did. Sometimes, a little too optimistic. I was getting comfortable, and I started drinking heavily again. One night, I decided to go for a little drive and got another driving under the influence. I didn't tell my boss what happened; I just told him we were moving back to Arizona, due to family issues. He offered me a position in Phoenix, doing the same thing I was doing in Philadelphia, just over the phone.

I crushed it, I was beating everyone out in the field, and I was only getting three appointments a day, and they were getting four. As senior reps, we were paid in three different ways; we were paid for selling machines, bonuses for going above and beyond, and residual income. My residuals were growing, and I sold my first portfolio for thirty thousand dollars.

I was 24 when I received that big check, and I sent that money to my grandparents to hold for me until I wanted to invest in something. One day, I made a promise to myself and said I will not work for anyone else except for who I am working for right now. I loved what I was doing, I mastered my craft, and I wasn't going to stop. At a company's Christmas party, my boss invited my parents, and I gave a speech.

It was my first time talking in front of that many people. I remember how proud my dad was of me for becoming a successful executive at such a young age. I was happy, healthy, and motivated, and I thought nothing could go wrong. A year later, my boss had a company meeting and let everyone know he was going a different route with the company. He laid off seventy-five percent of the company and offered all of the senior agents a severance pay or an opportunity to start our own processing company under his.

I was the only one out of seven of us to take the opportunity; everyone else took the severance pay, except one person who I regretfully made my partner. I ended up hiring two of the other seven to work for me. I learned right there that luck was being ready when the opportunity comes. I had money saved up from my portfolio that I sold and also borrowed some money from both my grandfather and father for equipment and other office expenses.

I remember listening to a CD in my car, I don't recollect who it was, but they said, "Do not let the company outgrow you; you have to outgrow the company." I didn't want to be stuck only learning what the company was teaching me. I wanted to learn how to become better than the company, so I was prepared and excited to start my own company when I was laid off. It was my time to run the show.

My First Business

In 2011, I started my first company; I made a lot of mistakes as a rookie business owner, some that I regret, but I learned from all of them. If you have never failed at anything in life, then you aren't growing. Many people let their failures detour them from their real goals, and others feed off of them. There are two types of people; people that get discouraged and give up too soon, and others fail, then adjust, and try again. I'm the second type of person. I saw something in this industry that was going to allow me to provide for my family forever.

The very first mistake was making someone my partner; I'm not saying that it's always bad to have a partner, but it pays to do some research, and if you do have a partner, make sure that they have the same work ethic and determination as you do. So, in the beginning, I told you that my grandfather and my father invested in the company, and I also put some of my own money into the company as well. My partner didn't contribute a dime. I made her 49% owner, and I own 51%.

However, she thought that she was inclined to get the same salary as I did. Not only was I the owner, but I was also still talking with owners and closing deals. She was supposed to be in charge of all the books and finances. Come to find out she wasn't paying any payroll taxes. The IRS doesn't play when you owe them money; they will put a lien on you, and they did just that with us. Our parent company saw that they put a lien on us and had to give our residual check to the IRS.

That happened one time, and our parent company did not like that, and ended up screwing us over and just taking our portfolio away from us. That was my first and biggest mistake I made as a business owner. The second mistake that I made was trying to grow too fast. We started off in a small office, it was one room, and we just put a bunch of desks against the wall, and my partner's and my desk were in the back. Within a year, we wanted to get bigger, so we went to an open space in the same office complex that was triple the size.

Needless to say, we ended up back in to the office we started in because the rent was just too expensive, and we weren't growing as fast as we thought we were. Another mistake is, every Friday, I would take all of my employees, and we would drink at the bar and play pool. Most nights were fun and harmless, but some nights I didn't even make it home to my wife.

Problems arose quickly in my household, and my wife ended up leaving me, taking the kids and the dog, leaving me with an empty house. I was drinking and partying and thought that just because I was taking care of my family financially, that was enough. My actions hurt my wife tremendously. I loved her very much, but I was selfish and stupid only thinking for myself. I was hurt inside, and I wanted to make things right with her. When my parent company decided to take our book of business, due to a garnishment from the IRS for nonpayment of payroll taxes, I had to make another choice, to continue with my partner and start over or shut the doors and start over alone.

I gave her an opportunity, so we could continue to grow our business. I wrote out a partnership agreement saying that she would get a certain salary and I would get a salary, plus anything I closed I would get a percentage. It was reasonable, and at this point, I was doing all of the selling because we ended up letting go of our other senior reps. She didn't want to sign it, so I closed down the doors and told everyone to stay home that we were done. I had to let the company go because of all the mistakes that I made. It was a learning experience, and sometimes, I wish I could go back and make those adjustments. But other times, I'm glad that I took that road. It made me a smarter and stronger business owner.

GOING BACK TO WORK

My wife and I knew we had to get away and out of the environment. We were in if we wanted to make things right. So we moved to San Diego to be closer to my family. Before we moved out there, I researched companies in San Diego that did merchant processing. I met up with a man named Kevin, who is now one of my business partners and a good friend.

I told him about my situation, showed him my business plan, and told him that I would be able to grow his company tremendously. He had an office in San Diego, and I brought my computers, phones, and game plan to his office. He let me have total freedom to do what I knew how to do best. He didn't charge me rent; we just split the cost of the employees and made money.

I was doing all of the closings in the beginning, but a year later, we hired someone to do the closing and had five employees setting appointments for that person. I was in training mode. I knew that if I could train more people that I could make more money. Things were going really good, and my wife and I were happy. We had a house, two cars, and three kids; I guess you could say we were living the American dream. Even though things were going well for us, I was at home with my friends that I grew up with, and when we get together, bad things seem to happen. I started to drink heavily again, and whenever I start to drink like that, I lose focus on what really matters. I started hanging out and staying out late with my friends again, not coming home all the time, and I was drunk from Friday night and all-day Saturday, as well as spent all day Sunday recovering. I was a weekend warrior, as they say.

I got my work done during the week and was making great money, but I wasn't taking care of my family emotionally. My wife was still hurt from what I did in Phoenix, and with me drinking and going out like I was, I lost her trust, and she ended up leaving me for a second time after a rough night. That night, I was at the bar and came home around two in the morning, plastered. We ended up getting into a fight, and she called the cops on me. I left the house and ended up getting another DUI.

This was my fourth DUI, so I thought for sure I was going to spend the next year of my life in prison, and so did she. She had her dad come from Chandler, Arizona, to pick her and the kids up and take them back. I was left with an empty house, with the Christmas decorations still up and my heart broken. I deserved it and spent the next year of my life trying to better myself as a person. It was the hardest year that I have ever had to endure.

I was twenty-nine years old, and I moved into my dad's house. I hadn't lived with him for twelve years since I was seventeen, and here I was about to be thirty years old living at home. It was depressing, and it was hard, but I had to deal with the consequences of my actions. I had a case pending and didn't know if I was going to jail or what was going to happen to me. I started praying, going to AA meetings, and trying to get my mind right.

For a year, I lived in San Diego with my dad, and my wife and kids lived with her parents in Chandler. I took trips out to Arizona for Christmas and random weekends. Being without my family was hands down the hardest thing that I have ever been through. I hired an attorney to handle my case, and I didn't have to go to court. He ended up making a plea agreement, and my sentence was ten days trash pickup and DUI classes. I completed my classes and community service immediately and was done within six months. I was done with San Diego once again; I had to get to my family. I decided to talk to my partner and told him my situation. My plan was to go to Arizona and open another office.

Life Now

In June of 2016, I moved to Chandler and opened a second office. I carried that momentum over to the new office, and I am continuing to grow my business

My wife, Annette Durden, and my four children, Isaiah Durden, Alyiah Durden, Sophiah Durden, Meiah Durden, and I are all currently living in Chandler Arizona.

Isaiah is 11 years old, is currently playing football, and just got a scholar-athlete award for having over a 3.75 GPA. Alyiah is 10 and is into Art, and both Isaiah and Alyiah will be running track in the winter. Sophia is 4 years old and is getting ready to start kindergarten. Meiah is 2, and she is our little trooper; she has a disease called cystic fibrosis, which affects her lungs. She is the happiest baby, and we are trying to stay positive through her journey. Annette is helping me grow my merchant service company and handling all the administrative work from home while taking care of the baby and the rest of us. She is the real deal, and if you are ever lucky enough to find someone that can handle everything that I put her through and stay, you better eventually get yourself together and show that person the most appreciation. Although I have made mistakes in my life, I have learned a lot, and I am most grateful for my family and friends that I made along the way.

How I made my first million

There are a lot of ways to sell; you have face to face, over the phone, internet sales and many more. I am going to give you a sales process that has worked for me and will work for you as well. This sales process can be done in person or over the phone. You can use this sales process with any product or service. It has made me over a million dollars and has given me a passive Income, so that I can work on my businesses, take vacations when I want, and spend quality time with my family without having to worry about if bills are going to get paid.

First of all you have to have a product or service to sale, if you don't have a product or service there are many out there. It doesn't have to be something you are passionate about, as long as you have your why in place; all you need is an opportunity, persistence, and drive.

You need three sets of scripts with rebuttals. First you need an opening script to get you to the right person, then an appointment script to get you the appointment, then a closing script to seal the deal. Once the script is written output it to the test. Get on the phones and start setting appointments for yourself, either in person or over the phone. Use the internet to generate leads, you can find residential or business leads free online. Once you've worked out all the kinks by yourself, you need to hire people to set appointments for you. Build it up until you can't fulfill all of the appointments. Then train someone to close the deals while you continue to close deals and give that person a percentage of the sale. Continue the process over and over again until you have an empire. I know it sounds simple but it's a long process that takes commitment and hard work. Anyone can do it and it doesn't matter what you are selling I know it will work.

-Scriptwriting

When writing a sales script the most important aspect is getting a hold of the right person, if you aren't talking to the right person you are wasting your time. So you have to write out an opening script. I like to lead in with an or question such as " is Fred there or is gone for the day " this doesn't allow a yes or no answer. Most of the time they will ask what it's about. Let them know what it is and it's important that you talk to him. If they aren't there try to get an alternate phone number, always leave a message if you can't get a hold of them, but make sure you follow back up with the people you leave messages with.

-Setting appointments.

When writing out your script get straight to the point. Say who you are and what you are calling about in the first sentence. The key is to get an appointment not sell to sell anything on the call. Qualify the person to see if the person is the right buyer for your products, ask questions but not too many you'll lose them. Once you qualify the buyer set the appointment for a presentation.

-Rebuttals

While in your beginning stage you are going to hear a lot of objections. Write down each objection that you hear. You will probably hear the same ones over and over again. Then go back and write out rebuttals for each objection. Rebuttals are when you give counter-arguments to an objection or disprove their statement. You should always be updating your rebuttals and mastering them to perfection.

-The close

Closing is an art and can be mastered by anyone. People will buy from you sometimes if they like your product, but many will buy from you if they like you and the product. Become a master of communication. When writing out your closing script, make sure you give benefits but don't show them the price until last. Pre-close, which means ask for the sale before giving the price. Recap everything you go over with the buyer and ask if there is anything holding them back from becoming your customer today. If they say yes, make sure you are addressing all of their concerns before moving to price. If they say no, then give them the price. If they don't buy from you then you know it's the price, and you didn't offer enough value.

In sales, it's a numbers game and you won't close every single deal, but that doesn't mean give up on it. Keep following up until they buy from you. If they didn't buy from you, then they bought from someone else, always keep that in mind.

Dear Reader,

Thank you for taking the time to read my book, I am truly grateful that you made a choice to better your life, that's the first step in the success process. I hope that you found inspiration in reading this book and it gave you a big push in the right direction. Please check out my website and reach out to me anytime. Don't forget to leave a review on amazon, and refer the book to family friends and loved ones.

Your Friend,

Ryan Durden

WWW.RYANDURDEN.COM

Made in the USA
Middletown, DE
28 February 2019